PE

KS2/3

AND
ROUS

THIRD
EDITION

N
E
S

LEAPFROGS

DAVI

Published in 2006 by A & C Black Publishers Ltd
38 Soho Square, London W1D 3HB
www.acblack.com

Third edition 2006
Second edition 2003
First edition 1995

ISBN-10: 0 7136 7726 0
ISBN-13: 978 0 7136 7726 3

A CIP record for this book is available from the British Library.

Cover illustration by Paul Oakley
Inside illustrations by Gaynor Berry and Eric Drewery

A & C Black uses paper produced with elemental chlorine-free pulp, harvested from managed sustainable forests.

Printed and bound in Great Britain by Caligraving Ltd, Thetford, Norfolk.

Contents

Introduction

The inclusion of Outdoor and Adventurous Activities (OAA) in three out of four key stages (KS) of the National Curriculum (NC) for PE is an indication of the value placed by leading educationalists, the Office for Standards in Education (OFSTED) and the Department for Education and Skills (DfES) on the undisputed benefits of stimulating experiences gained outside of the classroom in challenging learning situations. Indeed, as I write the DfES are presently engaged in a government enquiry, the 'Education outside the classroom' manifesto. The proposal is that every child is given at least one experience in each year of compulsory eduction. Such activities will call on the individual to overcome physical and emotional difficulties, work with and trust others, and develop a respect for the natural world.

The Programmes of Study (PoS) for KS3 OAA is less prescriptive than at KS2, providing scope for the teacher to cover aspects of the KS2 activities that may not have been pursued at KS2 through limitations in time or resources.

Although KS2 OAA is no longer a compulsory element of the PE National Curriculum, it has been favourably set as a 'teacher-friendly' option against swimming. Some schools will not be able to make provision for swimming due to restraints in an already overcrowded timetable and transport logistics to off-site pools. A similar scenario exists at KS3 where OAA appears as an option set against swimming and athletics. I hope that hard-pressed teachers of KS2 attempting to cope with NC PoS for a whole range of curricular disciplines will welcome this book as an aid in satisfying this aspect without undue complication. My philosophy has been to keep it simple, to make the information 'teacher-friendly'. I am sure teachers will find this work both great fun and rewarding to see the positive way in which children tackle the activities and respond to the adventure and challenge.

Where several activities are detailed for a particular PoS, the teacher can chose to do one or more to suit his or her own circumstances. The activities outlined have been designed to fulfil the PoS without the need to undertake specialised In-Service Training (INSET) or to acquire nationally recognised qualifications in hazardous OAA.

It is important to understand that OAA (encompassing recognised outdoor pursuits, adventure sports and development games) are a vital aspect of outdoor education in general. Outdoor education in its purest definition is any educational activity that takes place outside the formal classroom, a strategy for learning in all NC subjects, endorsed by the School Curriculum and Assessment Authority (SCAA), formerly the National Curriculum Council and now the Qualifications and Curriculum Authority (QCA).

The Institute for Outdoor Learning (IOL) – address on page 95 – is an organisation from which teachers of outdoor education can seek information and guidance. The National Association for Outdoor Education (NAOE), now the IOL, defined outdoor education as: 'A means of approaching educational objectives through guided, direct experience in the environment, using its resources as learning materials' (1970). Following the announcement of the foundation subjects, and as a result of considerable pressure from many outdoor education representatives, the Secretary of State for Education issued instructions to the SCAA working party for PE to advise on PoS related to OAA. In 1991 the DfES stated that:

'In OAA pupils apply physical and judgmental skills in different contexts, developing knowledge and experience of moving in different, challenging and changing environments.'

The proven educational benefits for pupils experiencing a course of this nature have been acknowledged for many years:

○ personal, moral and social development

○ increased understanding of and respect for the environment

○ improved health and satisfying use of leisure time from cultivating interests in adventure sports such as climbing, abseiling, mountaineering, paragliding, hang gliding, caving, canoeing, sailing, windsurfing, orienteering, mountain biking, walking, gliding, skiing, rafting, scuba diving, rowing, horse riding and angling (as recognised by the DfES).

The following outcomes in pupil development are all possible through involvement with OAA. (This list is useful at parents' evenings when attempting to justify the activities to sceptical parents!)

Development of:

○ character

○ self confidence

○ determination and perseverance

- self-discipline
- self-awareness and integrity
- tolerance of others
- social awareness and interest in the welfare of others
- unselfish, compassionate attitudes
- leadership
- initiative and self-motivation
- respect for the environment
- awareness of conservation and pollution issues
- community spirit
- humility and respect for others
- self-respect and dignity.

The ingredients of any outdoor adventure experience comprise of varying levels of psychological, physiological and technical expertise. These commodities may provide a useful means of assessment:

- the affective domain – feelings, emotions aroused through the activity (satisfaction, awe, joy, response to challenge); the PSHE (personal, social, health education) content

- psychomotor dexterity – hand–eye–brain co-ordination developed through the physical skill-based nature of some of the activities

- cognitive knowledge – acquired to solve problems, prepare and plan for journeys and activities.

Adventure-based activities rely on the presence of a physical or psychological challenge for pupils to overcome. The presence of a challenge implies the presence of risk, which in turn implies the presence of danger to some degree or other. Dangerous activities are hard to justify educationally unless one can show that all possible steps to eliminate the danger have been taken, and DfES/LEA recommended codes of practice are being followed.

In determining what constitutes an 'acceptable risk' one must analyse danger more thoroughly. In keeping with other PE activities it would be wise practice to have a Health and Safety policy for OAA and documented Risk Assessments for the activities undertaken. The HSE can be useful in this respect (see useful addresses on page 95). I have included a sample 'risk assessment' pro-forma on page 8. 'Dynamic' risk assessment is the on-going risk analysis taking place during the activity itself. You need to be one step ahead of the activity at all times and be constantly asking yourself 'what if?' Being in a position to act quickly and avoid mishap

is a key factor in avoiding problems. Subjective danger is that which can be controlled by the supervisor through correct choice of venue to suit the abilities of the participants, the assessment of weather and its effect on the activity, the correct application of safety techniques, good leadership, strict adherence to recommendations by relevant National Governing Bodies (NGBs) and, if appropriate, any Adventure Activities Licensing Authority (AALA) and LEA directives. Schools are not required to possess an AALA licence when providing activities for their own pupils. However, most LEA/Governing Authorities now accept that AALA recommendations and codes of practice should be used as a benchmark for safety in the activities. Objective danger is that which lies to some extent outside the control of the supervisor, e.g. a lightning strike, an avalanche, a rockfall, etc. However, even these events can be avoided by understanding the physical conditions associated with these phenomena. Clearly at KS2 and KS3 level the objective danger is minimal, whereas a Himalayan expedition represents obvious and ever-present dangers.

Furthermore, danger can be perceived as that which is deemed to be real and life-threatening, e.g. 'If you walk too close to the edge of that cliff you will fall', and that which is apparent to the individual but is not necessarily life-threatening, e.g. a pupil on the end of a climbing rope. The pupil may feel that if he slips he will fall to the ground, when in reality he should be held by the belayer(s) at the other end.

In staging adventure learning situations we should note that there are four recognised levels of adventure threshold which may be experienced by an individual. The point at which an individual will reach a particular threshold is peculiar to his or her experience, familiarity with the activity, training and understanding, personality, etc.

- **Level 1: Recreation** – little stimulation, boredom, arising out of an activity that has minimal challenge or enjoyment. For example, a group of 11-year-olds being led on a walk around the school premises with no pupil-based tasks.

- **Level 2: Adventure** – minimal arousal resulting from repetition or a challenge set well below the pupils' abilities. For example, a bouldering (low-level) climbing exercise on a frame or wall that does not call on the pupil to think about the correct moves to reach a predetermined point on the frame.

- **Level 3: Frontier adventure** – maximum arousal, full concentration and employment of mental and physical attributes to overcome a new, stimulating challenge. For example, a rope trail through a forest in darkness.

○ **Level 4: Misadventure** – genuine fear, anxiety, inability to cope with a very real danger that has arisen through an inappropriate challenge. For example, leading a group up or down a cliff face where the possibility of safeguarding a fall is impracticable.

Clearly then, pitching the activity at the appropriate level for a particular group can be an extremely difficult task. As the teacher acquires more experience and understanding of the group, then this task becomes more manageable.

In practice, with mixed ability groups it is not at all easy to cater for all thresholds. The more confident pupils can be given extra responsibility or asked to help others. **The golden rule is that the activity must be pitched at the level of the weakest group member**. I have attempted to help the supervising teacher in this respect through the format of the suggested activities in this book. For those teachers working with children with special needs, I have included a section with suggestions on how to cope with differing disabilities. However, I feel that specialist Special Educational Needs (SEN) teachers are better equipped to design their own strategies having seen what activities are possible to fulfil the PoS.

In writing this book I have tried to illustrate how the PoS for KS2 (and KS3) may be fulfilled effectively by non-specialist teachers without recourse to extensive (and expensive!) INSET to satisfy DfES/LEA Health and Safety codes of practice in recognised adventure sports such as climbing, canoeing, etc. However, if your school is in a position to offer such activities, either from within (if suitable resources and qualified staff are available) or through outside agencies, then the programme and its outcomes will be enhanced. In dealing with these hazardous adventure activities I have indicated what I would constitute a suitable strategy for teachers who fulfil their LEA's supervisory requirements.

Some LEAs will provide an 'in-house' system of training and accreditation at 'taster' level. Details can be obtained from your PE Advisor or General Education Inspector.

There is a wide range of adventure activities currently available through outside agencies and private country centres. The canoeing tragedy at Lyme Bay has served to highlight the fact that private centres do not necessarily have to comply with DfES recommendations. Following this tragedy, the DfES has stated that the responsibility for assessing the safety aspects of an outside agency lies solely with the school. I have therefore included a section on outside agencies – a checklist of good practices to look for when deciding to use these services.

It goes without saying that even with the limited exposure to danger that KS2 (and KS3) activities will present, the challenging nature of the activities must be acknowledged. It is most important for supervising staff to be alert to any possible hazards and plan accordingly. Strict regimes of discipline and organisation are essential. Further advice for each activity along with a general appraisal of what the teacher should consider with regard to safety and supervision is given throughout the book.

KS2 teachers may wish to explore and exploit the potential for learning with OAA from cross-curricular themes, e.g. a planned day of canoeing on a lake may relate to classroom studies on the 'water cycle'. I have indicated any possibilities for these links to take place in the activities described.

Finally, the strong links between OAA and residential experience deserve recognition and attention. Although there is no statutory requirement for a residential experience at KS2 (or KS3), a school may wish to pursue this further opportunity to promote PSHE. Residential experience requires children to adapt and respond to unfamiliar routines, environments and social groupings. Furthermore, a sense of purpose and focus of specific stimuli can be achieved in the rarefied atmosphere of a residential setting. When linked to residential experience, OAA can develop social learning skills through the challenging, team building, socially aware and interdependent nature of the situation, highlighting how an overnight standing camp, bivouac or stay in a youth hostel may be planned.

Finally, a government enquiry, set up to investigate health and safety relating to several recent tragedies involving swift water adventure activities, recommended that:

1 The LEA appoint a safety co-ordinator for all residential trips (an O.Ed Advisor).

2 That schools appoint a safety co-ordinator for all residential trips (EVC).

3 That all members of staff are equipped with a Residential Safety Handbook.

4 That all category 'C' visits are allowed to take place only with the approval of the O.Ed LEA advisor/safety officer.

A full list of category 'C' activities can be obtained from your LEA advisor or the DfES. I have indicated in this book the activities that require category 'C' approval.

The enquiry recommendations are part of the resulting DfES publication *Health and Safety of Pupils on Educational Visits* (HASPEV). See p. 95 for further details.

Risk Assessment

ACTIVITY: Y6/7 ORIENTEERING

IDENTIFIED HAZARDS	PEOPLE AT RISK
1 Getting lost	**1** Students
2 Stumbles and falls	**2** Students and teacher
3 Group getting split up	**3** Students
4 Water	**4** Students and teacher
5 Dehydration	**5** Students and teacher
6 Hypothermia/Hyperthermia	**6** Students and teacher
7 Exhaustion	**7** Students and teacher
8 Approached by strangers	**8** Students
9 Barbed wire, fences, twigs and vegetation	**9** Students and teacher
10 Dogs	**10** Students and teacher

EXISTING MEASURES IN PLACE	EXTRA PRECAUTIONS/MEASURES NEEDED
1 Pupils instructed to stay inside school grounds. Preliminary map and compass training etc.	**1** Contact numbers
2 First aid, survival blanket available with teacher. Emergency contact numbers	**2**
3 Instruct the group that they must stay together	**3**
4 Keep well away from rivers, lakes and ponds	**4** Water features fenced off
5 Carry water, drink regularly	**5**
6 Dress appropriately for the conditions	**6**
7 Stop and rest, sugary food available	**7**
8 Stay together, do not accept lifts or gifts such as sweets	**8**
9 Make students aware of these hazards and be on the lookout	**9**
10 Warn pupils not to encourage animals. Call for help	**10**

Record of Achievement

Physical Education – Key Stage 2 Outdoor and Adventurous Activities

Pupil _____

Key Stage Descriptions

A Take part in outdoor activity challenges, including following trails in familiar, unfamiliar and challenging environments

B Use a range of orienteering and problem-solving skills

C Work with others to meet the challenges

KS Descr.	Activity	Location	Date	Attainment (A–E)				Comments
				Y3	Y4	Y5	Y6	

Record of Achievement

Physical Education – Key Stage 3 Outdoor and Adventurous Activities

Pupil _____

Key Stage Descriptions

A Meet challenges in outdoor activities and journeys

B Use a range of orienteering and problem-solving skills and techniques in these challenges

C Identify the roles and responsibilities of individuals within a group when planning strategies

D Respond to changing conditions and situations

KS Descr.	Activity	Location	Date	Attainment			Comments
				Y7	Y8	Y9	

Self-assessment sheet

1 What has been the biggest contribution you have made during these activities?

2 What have you found the most difficult to cope with?

3 What do you think you have gained from the course?

4 What have you learned about your own capabilities?

5 How well do you feel you performed?

6 Is there anything you could have improved on?

7 Have you changed your views on other people in the group? If so, how and why?

8 Who in the group impressed you and why?

9 What have you learnt about working in a group?

10 What have been your group's greatest strengths and weaknesses?

11 Which activity have you enjoyed the most and why?

12 Which activity, if any, have you disliked and why?

The PoS attainment target and NC requirements

KS2

(A) **Take part in outdoor activity challenges, including following trails.**

(B) **Use a range of orienteering and problem-solving skills.**

(C) **Work with others to meet the challenges.**

Activity	POS covered
1 Scavenger hunts	b, c
2 Observation trails	a, b, c
3 Treasure hunts	a, b, c
4 Simple mapping exercises	a, b, c
5 Basic orienteering	a, b, c
6 Adventure games (smugglers, hide and seek, stalking, rope trails, blindfold trust games, blindfold confidence games)	a, c
7 Nature trails and scavenger hunts	a, b, c
8 Visits to the seaside (coastal activities)	a, c
9 Confidence courses and activity trails	a, c
10 Walks and rambles	a, c
11 Orienteering (advanced)	a, b, c
12 Camping and bivouacking	a, b, c
13 Problem-solving activities	a, b, c

KS3

(A) **Meet challenges in outdoor activities and journeys.**

(B) **Use a range of orienteering and problem-solving skills and techniques in these challenges.**

(C) **Identify the roles and responsibilities of individuals within a group when planning strategies.**

(D) **Respond to changing conditions and situations.**

Activity	POS covered
9 Confidence courses and activity trails	a
10 Walks and rambles	a, c, d
11 Orienteering (advanced)	a, b, c
12 Camping and bivouacking	a, c, d
13 Problem-solving activities	a, b, c

Attainment target

The attainment target (AT) for KS2/KS3 PE is the extent to which pupils fulfil the end of KS descriptions in the PoS, i.e. the levels 1–8.

Cross-curricular links/general teaching requirements

Along with other NC subjects I have tried to indicate links with the threads of citizenship, literacy, numeracy, inclusion (see p. 94), use of language, ICT and health and safety.

Assessment and planning

National Curriculum for PE

Main headings for considering progression and expectation.

The knowledge, skills and understanding are:

1 Acquiring and developing skills.

2 Selecting and applying skills, tactics and compositional ideas.

3 Knowledge and understanding of fitness and health.

4 Evaluating performance.

The treatment of the thorny subject of assessment and recording attainment doesn't have to be over-elaborate and time-consuming to be effective and representative of the PoS and AT. The strategies of planning–performing–evaluating lend themselves well to the activities prescribed in this book.

To recap, let us not forget that attainment in PE is the extent to which pupils fulfil the end of KS descriptions in the PoS. In addition to this, let us not forget that when we look for criteria to assess in OAA, we can analyse the activity in terms of its cognitive knowledge, psychomotor dexterity and affective emotional response.

Cognitive knowledge can be assessed through the responses to practical assignments offered to the pupils, as well as through the photocopiable pupil resource sheets supplied. Psychomotor dexterity is closely linked to performing. A number of the activities in KS2 (and KS3) will require these skills if the pupil is to succeed in the tasks. Suitable activities include climbing, activity circuits, confidence courses and some of the adventure games. In describing and recognising his response and performance in the activities, the pupil will be satisfying any need for assessment in the affective domain.

Above all, the assessment scheme should be simple to implement and of use to upper school teachers who will be pursuing OAA at KS3 and KS4.

A sample risk assessment sheet appears on page 8. Sample record of achievement sheets appear on pages 9 and 10, an example of a self-assessment sheet on page 11. The skills can be taken from the aims of each activity, e.g. camping and bivouacking – camping skills; ability to work with others.

Planning

The following headings have been used to help with planning schemes of work:

1 Assessment – how are we going to measure achievement?

2 Cross-curricular links.

3 Resources – what equipment is needed.

4 Extension and enrichment (including homework).

5 Vocabulary – the key words.

6 Aim – what are the hopeful outcomes of the activity?

7 Expectations

8 Health and Safety

9 Core tasks

10 Objectives

11 Activities

Within teacher's guidance notes. If further guidance is needed visit www.nc.uk.net.

Scavenger hunts

KS: 2

PoS: b and c

Aim: to develop observation skills and search strategies

Time required: 30–50 minutes

Location: school playground; school fields

Resources: coloured marker discs or similar; possibly cards with names of stations written on them

Target group: 7–8-year-olds. Class of 30 working in groups of 4 or 5

Teacher's guidance notes

Scavenger hunts will appeal to younger children's inquisitive nature and desire to explore. They can be linked to search and rescue techniques used by rescue organisations. The pupils are asked to work together as a group to find a set number of items within a defined area. You may wish to do some follow-up work on the rescue services. The children could be told what services are available – the telephone directory employs good graphics to depict the various agencies.

The focus for the hunt can be as simple as coloured markers (different colours to be collected). Markers can be situated in as many different stations as their colours, i.e. four colours, four stations.

The first group back with a complete set of markers wins, although you may feel that the competitive element is undesirable. Don't put markers in places of danger, places where children could fall or run into awkward objects.

It may be wise for the first hunt to be relatively straightforward, asking the pupils to collect one marker and informing them where it is hidden. Tell the children that they must move quietly through the school.

Assessment: assess results of hunt, questioning, feedback

Cross-curricular links: Citizenship; Health and Fitness; ICT

Pupil resources: none

Extension and Enrichment: find out about the various Search and Rescue Services available to persons in the UK, and how they are funded

Vocabulary: search, rescue, markers, station

Observation trails

KS: 2

PoS: a, b and c

Aim: to develop observation skills

Time required: 30–50 minutes

Location: school grounds

Resources: waymarker cards with arrows

Target group: 7–8-year-olds. Class of 30 working in groups of 4

Teacher's guidance notes

Observation trails follow waymarked routes in a similar way to those found on nature trails in forested areas or other areas of public countryside recreation. If a visit to such an area is possible, then the activity will be stimulating and rewarding for the pupils. However, I suggest that each group is supervised closely by an adult.

The same aims can be achieved within the school grounds by providing homemade way-markers for the children to follow. Bright backgrounds and the size and direction of the arrows should be given a good deal of thought. The pupils could be involved in repairing the arrows themselves. Staff could fix them to posts with pins, sticky tape, etc.

Set the course up and ask pupils to look for certain items, such as the number of trees on the trail; the number of red doors you pass; the number of houses you can see. Pupils can record their results on a sheet of paper and hand it in at the end for checking.

As with all activities involving journeys around the school, make sure that the children understand that they should not enter other classes or disturb fellow pupils.

The course should be designed so that the pupils can spot the next arrow before leaving the previous, to avoid getting lost and straying into potentially dangerous areas.

Assessment: examine results, questioning, feedback

Cross-curricular links: Citizenship; Health and Fitness; Environment; ICT

Pupil resources: none

Extension and Enrichment: find out (possibly through the internet) the waymark symbols used on a long-distance footpath such as the Pennine Way

Vocabulary: waymarkers

Treasure hunts

KS: 2

PoS: a, b and c

Aim: to develop expertise in following graphical symbols; to provide pupils with an activity which will encourage a sense of discovery and exploration

Time required: 30–50 minutes

Location: school grounds

Resources: treasures; graphical instructions; plotting compasses; bar magnets

Target group: 7–8-year-olds. Class of 30 working in groups of 4

Teacher's guidance notes

Treasure hunts are a stimulating activity for young people, especially if the treasure is worth hunting for! Possible treasures could include sweets, chocolate bars, fruit, etc. Try to arrange for different treasure locations so that each group has a different journey and thus different route-finding problems.

Start with treasure hunts that have simple instructions such as left, right, forwards, backwards. Pupils should be interested as to what is meant by these commands, and be able to identify the commands on the instruction sheet:

Practise these movements until everyone is moving correctly. You could attempt to stage a marching course.

Issue pupils with treasure hunt details and discuss what is meant by a 'pace', i.e. L–R–L = 3 paces (keep it simple).

Pupils are to return to base with treasure as proof of discovery. Advanced learning could relate to the eight points of a compass. A large visual aid could be helpful here to show the eight points. Show the pupils how to turn the direction symbol until it lines up with the North-pointing end of a

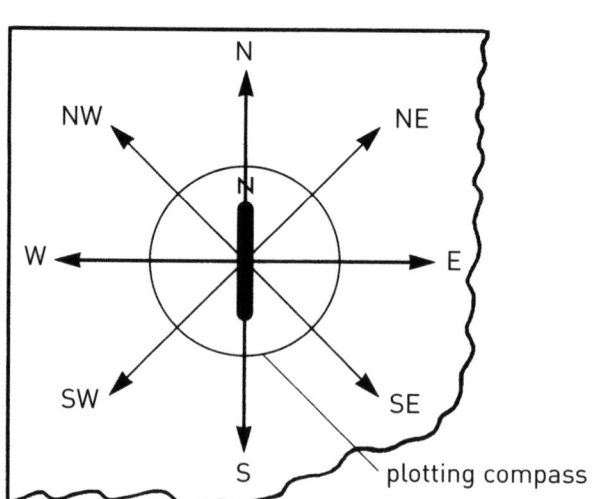

plotting compass

plotting compass needle. Discuss the fact that the compass needle always points North because of an invisible attracting force known as magnetism. If possible, put two bar magnets together to show the force of attraction.

Show them how to keep turning the sheet until North lines up. Now the instructions can be given in terms of the eight points of the compass and paces.

KS2

Assessment: observation of treasures, questioning, feedback

Cross-curricular links: Citizenship; Health and Fitness; Environment; Science; Geography; ICT

Pupil resources: instructions

Extension and Enrichment:

1 Find out about a ship's compass using library resources, CD roms, etc.

2 How did the old mariners navigate using the compass and stars?

Vocabulary: commands, pace, compass, magnetism

Simple mapping

KS2

KS: 2

PoS: a, b and c

Aim: to develop observation skills and convert information gained in the field

Time required: 30–50-minute map-making sessions, plus time for gathering information in the field

Location: classroom, gymnasium and local sites

Resources: pens, pencils, colours, tracing paper, clipboards

Target group: 7–8-year-olds. Class of 30 working individually

Teacher's guidance notes

Younger pupils can begin with a familiar environment such as the classroom.

1 The class could gather around a display of shaped blocks, a model of a building or something similar, and try to draw the layout as they see it from their viewpoint. Although all the 'maps' will be different, they are all correct. Now place another object in the display and ask the pupils to mark its position on their maps with an 'X'. Finish with a game of 'follow the leader' in which the teacher moves the figure's path of travel on the children's maps.

2 Prepare a set of maps showing the centre of the classroom and a piece of furniture or object marked at some other location. Pupils are to locate the object and find the coded letter, return to the teacher and attempt another map. This activity could be repeated in the gymnasium.

3 The teacher can then go on to ask pupils to imagine that they are looking down on the room.

Ask the pupils to visualise how the room would look from above. This is the principle behind a map. Pupils can trace the symbols for the room components and transfer them on to their plan. As with the previous activities, there need not be any reference to scale. The outline plan of any classroom may need to be altered to accommodate any irregularities in the shape of the room that do not correspond to the rectangular shape given on the photocopiable sheet.

4 Further activities can include walks to local sites, asking the pupils to record the shape of their journey on a blank sheet. Then ask them to make a larger, neater copy back at school. A useful road safety lesson can also be undertaken if the route chosen takes the pupils to places where the road signs on the other blank sheet are encountered. A clipboard is essential for these activities. So is dry weather if you are to have a sporting chance of disseminating the information on return to school.

Assessment: examine the finished plans and maps

Cross-curricular links: Environment; Geography; ICT

Pupil resources: see worksheets

Extension and Enrichment: find out about different types of map e.g. Town Street plan, O.S., etc. Use the internet to find out about map making

Vocabulary: map, symbol, plan

Making a map

Name _____

Make a plan of your classroom in the box below. Trace the symbols on to your plan in their correct position.

	symbol			**symbol**	
desk			window		
table			blackboard		
chair			cupboard		
door			bookshelf		
			any other items?		

If you have time, use different colours to show the symbols more clearly. We call this a 'key' or 'legend'.

A walk from school

Name_____

We are going to walk from school to _ _ _ _ _ _ _ _ _ _ _ _ _ _ _

Draw the route on this sheet. Then copy it out more accurately on a larger sheet of paper back at school.

church

police station

fire station

school

supermarket

park

my house

Look for these traffic signs on your journey to _ _ _ _ _ _ _ _ _ _ _ _ _ _ _ _ _ _ _

Mark your route plan with the number of the traffic sign. Back at school, trace the symbols on to the larger map.

1

What does it mean?

_ _ _ _ _ _ _ _ _

2

What does it mean?

_ _ _ _ _ _ _ _ _

3

What does it mean?

_ _ _ _ _ _ _ _ _

4

What does it mean?

_ _ _ _ _ _ _ _ _

5

What does it mean?

_ _ _ _ _ _ _ _ _

6

What does it mean?

_ _ _ _ _ _ _ _ _

Orienteering (basic)

KS: 2

PoS: a, b, and c

Aim: to introduce the sport of orienteering; to develop orientation skills using simple, pictorial maps and large scale plans

Time required: 30–35 minutes

Location: school grounds

Resources: 3D maps, painted boards

Target group: 7–8-year-olds. Class of 30 working in groups of 4

Teacher's guidance notes

In this section we are attempting to begin the process of relating a map to the surroundings – a basic navigational skill which forms the cornerstone of the most demanding navigational situations, e.g. Duke of Edinburgh Award Gold Expeditions.

The maps should be simplistic in design, of large scale and preferably three-dimensional. A simple plan of the school can be converted quite easily into a 3D map with a little imagination and use of simple projection.

A 3D map forms a useful halfway house, a transitional step for the pupils to grasp the relevant concepts before moving on to the use of aerial plans and Ordnance Survey maps in KS2.

Once competence has been achieved with a 3D map, it should be possible to move on to simple aerial plans. The maps should show clearly the features that the pupils can easily identify such as the school entrance, gymnasium, classrooms, etc. Do not produce a map with superfluous detail that will clutter and confuse. The pupils should be able

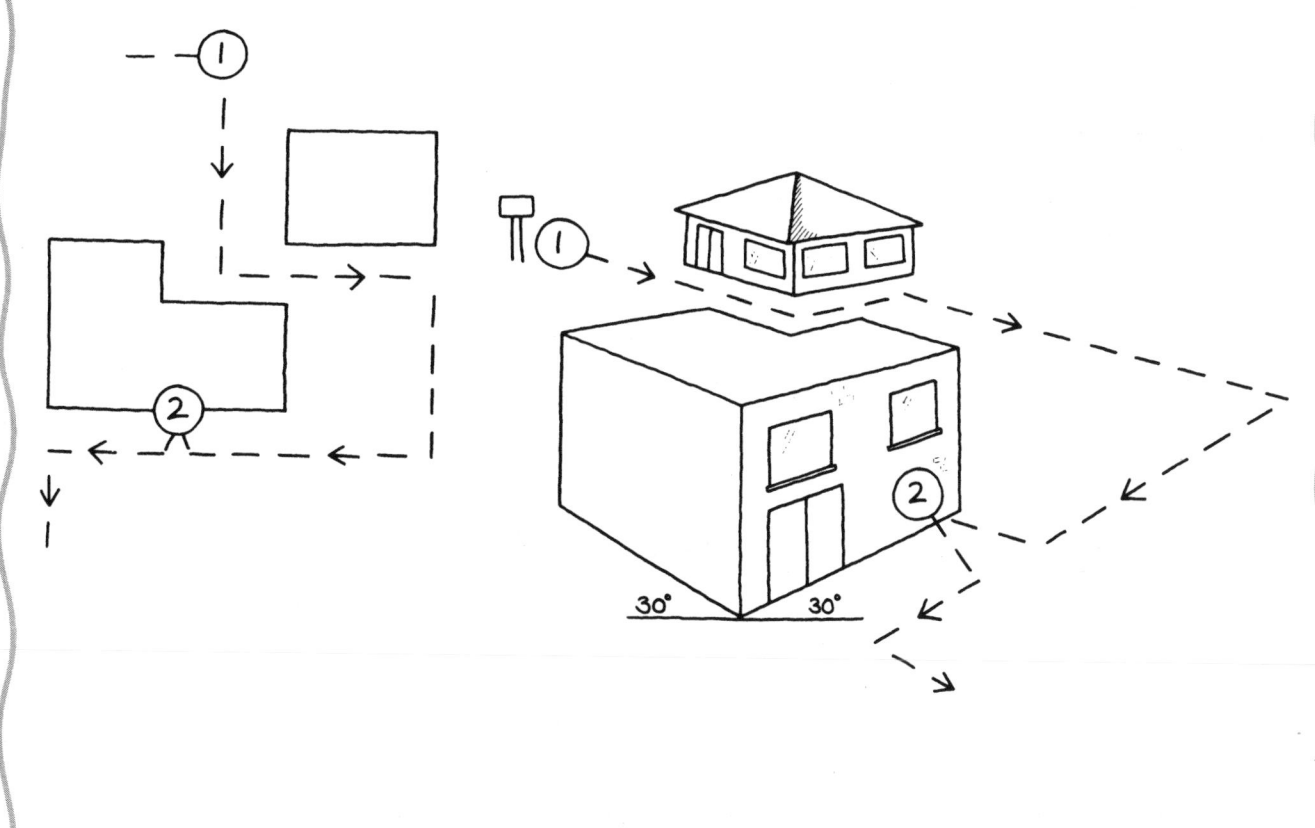

KS2

to see clearly the paths that they must take to find the orienteering markers (these can take the form of painted boards with an animal picture or something similar for them to identify) and complete the course.

Orienteering is a leisure activity in which participants have a map showing control points. They go to the control points, find the marker board and record the information on it. Sometimes they race against each other to see who can find them the fastest.

The pupils must be shown how to set the map, i.e. turn the map so that it lines up with the features they can see in front of them.

Do not mention scale at this stage of learning other than to say that everything on the map is a miniature version of its actual size.

You could also ask pupils to measure the length of the course by using pacing as in 'treasure hunts' activity (page 16).

Finally, remind pupils of out of bounds, and quiet rules as in other activities.

Assessment: examine the results

Cross-curricular links: Citizenship; Health and Fitness; Environment; ICT; Numeracy

Pupil resources: none (teacher to produce own map and result sheet)

Extension and Enrichment: where can you find out more about the sport of orienteering?

Vocabulary: 3D orientation, setting the map, orienteering, control point, aeriel

Adventure games — smugglers; stalking; hide and seek

KS: 2

PoS: a, c

Aim: to develop observational and listening skills; create opportunities for initiative; have fun and adventure and thereby develop oneself; to reinforce attributes in teamwork and group co-operation

Time required: most activities described can be pursued within a 30–35-minute period

Location: woodland

Resources: activity (a) smugglers – containers filled with loot, rope to mark the 'den', whistle, detention compound; activity (b) stalking – none; activity (c) hide and seek – none

Target group: 7–8-year-olds

Teacher's guidance notes

These games will encourage the pupils to move quietly and work together using sign language to outwit their opponents. Dark clothing and possibly army black-up for the face can add to the sense of adventure and fun.

a *Smugglers:* two teams of 4 or 5 set up their dens approximately 50 metres away in an area of dense woodland. The den should be marked with a rope laid out into a square approximately 10 by 10 metres. This size will give the opponents a sporting chance of penetrating the compound without being caught. Both teams not only have the problem of defending their own den, but they must attempt to infiltrate and capture the other team's treasure, e.g. bars of chocolate. If detected, the pupil caught must be escorted back to a detention point by one of the 'observers'. Decide on a time limit for the game (a whistle is useful for this purpose), after which the result is decided by the number of successful entries into the opponents' den. Each time a group member is successful, he/she can be exchanged for treasure at the conclusion of the game.

b *Stalking:* teach the children various ways of stalking and creeping up on targets without being detected. Display techniques such as pulling themselves along on their stomachs, hands and knees making shuffling movements, etc. Split the group into pairs; each member of the pair should go to opposite ends of the woodland. The aim is to sneak up on the partner and touch them on the shoulder before they are spotted. Note that children's clothing will become very dirty and possibly torn. It is a good idea to warn pupils of the possibility of twigs penetrating the eye, thorns in fingers, nettle stings, etc. A set of protective glasses, leather gardening gloves and old clothing are recommended. The activity could be followed by a group session in which the group attempts to stalk deer or other elusive forest fauna.

c *Hide and seek:* no introduction is needed to this established adventure game other than to comment that ground rules should be laid down regarding the limits of where the pupils may hide, places of danger to avoid (such as up trees and down holes), etc. Decide on a hiding and searching time limit, whereupon the victim has won if not found. Change roles.

Assessment: direct observation

Cross-curricular links: Citizenship; Environment; ICT; Language

Pupil resources: none

Extension and Enrichment: awareness of these skills as part of armed services training. The work of Army/Air Cadet forces, etc.

Vocabulary: den, fauna, loot, detention, compound

Adventure games — rope trails

KS: 2

PoS: a, c

Aim: to develop confidence and trust in others; to appreciate the sense of sight and gain a better understanding of those who are blind

Time required: 30–50 minutes, depending on the length of the trail and the number in the group

Location: school playground or field

Resources: a length of rope and possibly some climber's slings (simple rope slings will suffice) and karabenas (form of snap link); blindfolds

Target group: 9–11-year-olds

Teacher's guidance notes

Set up the rope so that the pupils must negotiate a number of obstacles. All obstacles should be positioned a safe height from the ground, generally less than a metre. Avoid big drops and sharp, pointed obstacles. Take into account any slippery surfaces as well when designing the course.

If you wish, the rope may be tied off at various points with a figure-of-eight knot, clipped into a climber's karabena and doubled sling, which may

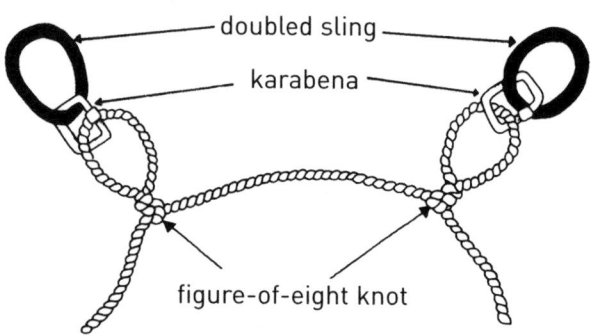

- doubled sling
- karabena
- figure-of-eight knot

be threaded through around a post or bar, or simply looped over the top of a post. This will enable the course to be more tortuous and disorientating.

Obstacles could range from natural features such as fallen trees, logs, fences and small ditches, to steps to hurdle, benches, vaulting box, horse, high jump mat and bar. Try to design a course in which the pupils can go under, through and round obstacles as well as over them.

When the course is ready (the pupils can help set it up), number the pupils 1 or 2. All number 1s are blindfolded (use anything that is available such as scarves, lengths of material, etc.). Pair off a number 1 with a number 2. The number 2s offer only verbal assistance in guiding their partner around the course and over the obstacles. Verbal assistance can relate to the nature of the obstacle and how best to negotiate it. On completion of the course, the pupils can swap roles. Design a new course if time permits.

Assessment: direct observation, questioning, feedback

Cross-curricular links: Health and Fitness; Citizenship; Language

Pupil resources: none

Extension and Enrichment: awareness of Adventure Centres and specialised facilities for persons with disabilities

Vocabulary: rope, karabena, guide, blindfold, disability

Adventure games – blindfold trust games

KS: 2

PoS: a, c

Aim: as in the previous activity, also to accommodate each other's performance

Time required: 30–50 minutes

Location: playground or school field

Resources: various obstacles as in the previous activity, blindfolds

Target group: 9–11-year-olds

Teacher's guidance notes

a Guiding one another round an obstacle course. This is basically the same as the previous activity, but with no rope to guide the pupils. It will encourage the assistants to provide more accurate, detailed verbal instructions to guide successfully. New commands of left, right, forwards, backwards can be introduced.

b A variation of the above activity is to have a group of pupils moving together, either holding hands or attached to a rope at, say, one-metre intervals via a large figure-of-eight loop, which they can step into to form a waist tie. Prepared ropes with the loops already tied can save a great deal of time. The pupil at the front of the group is the leader, whose task is to coach and lead the rest of the group over the course. The remainder of the group are blindfolded.

Yet another variation is to remove the blindfolds and get the group to move as a team, as smoothly as possible.

Assessment: direct observation, questioning, feedback

Cross-curricular links: Health and Fitness; Citizenship; Language

Pupil resources: none

Extension and Enrichment: closing ones eyes and listening to the sounds around you

Vocabulary: rope, karabena, guide, blindfold, senses

Adventure games — blindfold confidence games

KS: 2

PoS: a, c

Aim: to overcome shyness and develop communication skills between pupils

Time required: 30–50 minutes

Location: school playground

Resources: blindfolds

Target group: 9–11-year-olds. Class of 30 working in groups of 4, then 10

Teacher's guidance notes

These activities can be a lot of fun for pupils. As with other blindfold activities, the children can come to appreciate the gift of sight and become more aware of the difficulties experienced by those who are blind.

1 Line pupils up and number them 1-2-3-4, 1-2-3-4, etc. Issue blindfolds and ask the group to disperse in the playground. Place blindfolds over eyes, and inform the number 1s that they are sheep. They may only make the sound of a sheep. Demonstrate noise. Inform the number 2s that they are cows, number 3s that they are

pigs, and number 4s that they are donkeys. Now each group member must find one another using the animal sound only.

2 Number pupils 1-2-3, etc. up to a maximum of 10. Issue blindfolds. Ask the pupils to disperse to form a circle and hold hands (one pupil can remain outside the circle with a blindfold on and guide the others). Now all must put on blindfolds and convert their circle into a straight line where all pupils are in numerical order, i.e. 1 first, 10 last.

Assessment: direct observation, questioning, feedback

Cross-curricular links: Citizenship; Health and Fitness

Pupil resources: none

Extension and Enrichment: closing one's eyes and concentrating on the smells around you

Vocabulary: blindfold, circle, senses

Nature trails and scavenger hunts

KS: 2

PoS: a, b, c

Aim: to provide a stimulating way in which to learn about a specific environment; to develop observational and searching strategies

Time required: ideally a whole day offsite visit, where the activity takes anything from an hour to half a day

Location: coastal, country or town parks, forestry commission sites

Resources: trail/hunt information material providing details of subjects under scrutiny; pens, pencils, clipboards; weatherproofing clear plastic bags or covering

Target group: 10–11-year-olds

Teacher's guidance notes

A nature trail quiz or scavenger hunt can be an effective means of increasing children's awareness of a particular environment. The exploration and discovery inherent in the activity will capture the imagination of the children and stimulate their natural instinct for adventure.

The quiz/hunt should have a clearly defined focus, ideally linked to preliminary classroom studies which may have been undertaken prior to the activity. Three examples are offered:

1 a trail quiz based on a country park which has developed a woodland habitat from earlier quarrying activity;

2 a marine scavenger hunt that could be part of a visit to the seaside (combined with Visits to the seaside – see page 29);

3 based on a town 'pocket' park with ironstone quarrying connections and a history of habitation by earlier civilisations, it involves simple map reading, observation and recording.

A simple map, such as those shown in the worksheet, may be useful to indicate the location of answer material. A quiz that includes a scavenger element – hunting for specimens – will add extra spice and fun to the proceedings. Take care, however, not to abuse environments by pillaging resources such as rock specimens, flowers, etc., unless permission has been granted and they can be taken without harming the environment. This can form a nice conservation issue to take up with the pupils.

As with orienteering, close supervision of the pupils may not always be possible. Therefore, safeguards should be undertaken to ensure that the environment is safe. Pupils should work in groups of 3 or 4, with a watch to enable them to return to base promptly, and knowledge of what to do in an emergency (see Planning a visit on pages 81–5). Alternatively, it may be wise to restrict the activity to a small area in which close supervision is possible.

Assessment: direct observation of teamwork skills; analysis of recordings, questioning, feedback

Cross-curricular links: Geography; History; Health and Fitness; Science; Technology; ICT

Pupil resources: *see* worksheet

Extension and Enrichment: find our where the nearest Country Park/Nature Trail is to your home

Vocabulary: nature trail, country park, woodland, environment, pocket park, history, quarry, civilisation, specimen, exploration

Nature trail

Hunsbury Hill Country Park

N

0   ¼   ½

kilometres

- - - - - footpaths

railway shed

station platform

HILL FORT

play area

X

triangulation station

picnic tables

B

adventure fort

C

D

Danes Camp Way

Nature Hill Road

Towcester Road A43

Mere Way

YOU ARE HERE

MEET HERE

○ All groups to visit location X – answer questions

○ Do not cross any main roads

○ Use the footpaths only

Checkpoints:

A *Bridge* – How many vertical bars does the bridge have?

B *Viewpoint stone* – How many picnic tables are there here?

C *Adventure fort* – List the types of playground equipment.

D *Railway terminus* – Work out the length of the railway platform using paces.

Questions to be answered at location X:

1 How big is the hill fort?

2 How old is the hill fort?

3 Who built the hill fort?

4 What material has been quarried in this area?

5 What did the early inhabitants of the hill fort store in pits?

6 In the nineteenth century, the railway you have seen was built. What do you think it was used for?

Visits to the seaside

KS: 2

PoS: a, c

Aim: to increase awareness of the coastal environment and marine ecosystems

Time required: preferably 3–8 hours

Location: coastal areas protected by the National Trust, country parks and coastal footpaths, ideally away from seaside resorts. Coastline should be easily accessible and offer opportunities to explore rock pools, mussel beds, etc. There should be no dangerous currents or places where the incoming tide may cut off pupils and sweep them out to sea. Steeply shelving beaches with dangerous undertows must also be avoided. See pages 86–91

Resources: marine organism identification sheets, graph paper, clipboards, quadrats, transect lines

Target group: 10–11-year-olds

Teacher's guidance notes

The dangers of school children undertaking activities on coastlines were highlighted by the Land's End tragedy. Choose your day and location carefully (see pages 86–91).

Everyone enjoys a visit to the seaside, especially pupils who live some distance away inland. It can be a stimulating experience, particularly if the coastline is relatively remote and rugged.

Preliminary classroom work relating to the seashore environment and the seashore code, and visits to the seaside should be undertaken prior to the visit.

There are a number of physical activities one can pursue, such as exploring caves, follow-the-leader and scrambling (see pages 86–91), in addition to less active sessions such as scavenger hunts, cooking freshly caught fish (purchased earlier from fishermen) and beach transects. Other activities might include a visit to a local 'sea life' centre.

1 *Scavenger hunt*: The tide must be at low water. Pupils are given a well-defined area, visible by the staff from a suitable vantage point, and an identification sheet. They are asked to bring back a specimen of each species detailed. On a simple outline plan of the area they can mark where they found the specimen. By comparing plans it may be possible for pupils to work out that different specimens live at different parts of the inter-tidal cycle.

2 *Transect*: Pupils are given a blank profile for each location, a quadrat (a measuring square) and a transect line. Specimens are counted and plotted on the graphs for each square metre along the line from low water to high.

Assessment: physical activities; direct observation. Environmental activities; worksheets, graphs, feedback, questioning

Cross-curricular links: Science; Environment; Conservation; Geography; ICT; Numeracy; Health and Safety

Pupil resources: see worksheets

Extension and Enrichment:

1 Where are the 'sea-life' centres?

2 Where is the nearest coastal resort to where you live?

Vocabulary: transect, quadrat, sewage, industrial waste, hypothermia, conservation, marine, seashore, coast, species, cave, tide, cliff, cove, pollution, high water, low water, beach, current, flood, pier, breakwater, rip, undertow, coasteering

Visits to the seaside

Name _____

- ○ The seashore can be a great place to have fun and adventure. Your teacher may be able to arrange a visit to undertake a marine scavenger hunt, trail quiz or coastal walk.

- ○ Coastal walks, along the top of cliffs or along beaches, can involve exploring coves and caves, scrambling over large rocks or traversing at the base of cliffs, and can be very exciting.

- ○ What else could we do? We might try cooking over an open fire or even spending the night on the beach or in a cave. This is known as 'bivouacking'.

- ○ We must respect the power of the sea and be wary of the dangers that can be present at the seashore.

- ○ The sea rises up the beach and falls away again every six hours to create a 'tide'. The highest point the water reaches is known as 'high water'.

   What is the lowest point known as? _____

   The tide is biggest when there is a full moon and smallest when the moon is at half phase.

- ○ The wind causes the waves that crash against the beach.

Marine life identification chart

Name _____

GROUP 1

EGG WRACK
(% cover per m² transect)

COMMON PERIWINKLE
(full size, black or beige)

COMMON WHELK
(full size, look for underside slit)

GROUP 2

LIMPET
(beige, conical shell)

ROUGH PERIWINKLE
(full size, red to black, look for
horizontal ridges on shell)

FLAT WRACK
(% cover)

GROUP 3

BARNACLE
(% cover)

FLAT PERIWINKLE
(full size, variable colour –
yellow, orange, green)

CHANNEL WRACK
(% cover)

Visits to the seaside

Name _____

Blank profile – exposed beach   GROUP _____ TIME _____ DATE _____

100 ┬
 50 ┤
  0 ┤
 50 ┤
  0 ┤
 50 ┤
  0 ┤
HW   → LW

SPECIES 1 SPECIES 2 SPECIES 3

☐ SCALE: 1 GRID ☐ REPRESENTS 1 QUADRAT

Blank profile – sheltered beach   GROUP _____ TIME _____ DATE _____

100 ┬
 50 ┤
  0 ┤
 50 ┤
  0 ┤
 50 ┤
  0 ┤
HW   → LW

SPECIES 1 SPECIES 2 SPECIES 3

☐ SCALE: 1 GRID ☐ REPRESENTS 1 QUADRAT

The seashore safety code (1)

Name_____

Study with your teacher the safety points listed below. Fill in the missing blanks and create an information poster by making drawings on a separate piece of paper to illustrate the safety rules. The first one has been done for you.

○ Don't ignore warning signs.

○ Beware of becoming stranded by incoming tides. If caught, try to climb above the high water mark. Beware of going into caves that might flood.

○ Don't go in or on the water in windy weather. Why? _____

_____

○ Don't swim if a red flag is flying. Only swim on beaches patrolled by lifeguards.

○ Red and yellow flags mean that lifeguards are on patrol and that it is safe to swim.

The seashore safety code (2)

Name_____

○ Don't swim near pipes, rocks, piers or breakwaters. Pipes that lead into the sea often carry sewage and industrial waste. Pollution of the sea has become a worrying problem and a number of surfers and regular bathers have suffered with intestine infections. Clean beaches are given an award – look for the flag below.

Can you think of other ways in which the marine environment is being polluted?

How do you think this might be affecting the creatures that live in the sea and people like fishermen who earn their living from the sea?

Seawatch is a conservation body that is dedicated to protecting the marine and coastal environment. They have a number of Sea Life Centres where you can see the creatures of the sea close up. Your teacher may be able to arrange a visit to one for you.

○ Make sure that you know what's beneath the surface. Why? _____

_____

○ Learn how to help someone in trouble. Learn basic lifesaving and rescue skills. Ring 999 and ask for the coastguard in an emergency.

○ Don't let yourself get too cold in the water. You may get cramp or hypothermia. Wear a wetsuit if you are going to be in the water for a long time (e.g. surfing, snorkelling).

The seashore safety code (3)

Name _

○ Don't swim after a big meal.

○ Beware of 'rip currents'. These are strong currents that can carry you out to sea. If you are caught in a rip, try to swim parallel to the shore until you are clear of it.

○ Always swim parallel to the shore.

○ Don't take lilos and inflatables on to the sea when the tide is going out, near rip currents, or when the wind is blowing offshore.

What does 'blowing offshore' mean? _

_ _

○ Keep well clear of boats.

○ Beware of sitting under cliffs. The rocks above may be loose.

○ On some beaches there can be strong undertows. Only go into the sea from beaches that are gently sloping or are approved for water activities. Never go out in rough conditions.

○ Beware of going too close to the edge of cliffs. Keep to paths and well away from cliff edges, especially in wet, windy conditions. Watch out for gusts of wind that could carry you over the edge.

○ Don't try to climb up or down cliffs unless you are with an experienced rock climber. Scrambling along the base of cliffs or over large rocks on the beach (under the supervision of your teacher) can be great fun as long as you don't climb too high. Wear a helmet. Make sure that the rocks are not loose and that you are not going to be cut off by the tide. 'Coasteering' is an exciting adventure activity which combines climbing skills with swimming and jumping into the sea; however, you need to wear a buoyancy aid or lifejacket and a wetsuit. You must be properly supervised for your own safety.

Confidence courses and activity trails

KS: 2/3

PoS: KS2: a, c; KS3: a

Aim: to develop confidence in one's own abilities and overcome challenging physical problems

Time required: 60 minutes to half a day

Location: school grounds, country parks*, town parks*, forestry recreation areas*

Resources: ropes, logs, planks, posts, climbing nets, gymnasium equipment, pipes, tunnels, totem climbing poles, stepping stones or blocks

Target group: 8–13-year-olds (according to course difficulty)

Teacher's guidance notes

A confidence or assault course is a trail which requires the student to undertake a number of physical tasks. These may involve an element of risk, suitably safeguarded by safety lines or on-the-spot supervision (spotting). Courses of this nature are often to be found at activity centres and army barracks. A growing number are being established at country/forestry recreation sites. Adventure playgrounds in municipal parks are another resource which could be utilised, but a more inventive approach may be necessary here since the park may be familiar to the children. Setting the children tasks on climbing frames, devising activity circuits or utilising trees and bushes (without trespass or damage) may be effective.

On-site confidence courses can be set up in the gym or on the school fields using normal gymnasium equipment. Transporting a log or bench over the course is another option available (assessment in teamwork skills can also take place here).

If a basic strategy of balancing and climbing over, under and through obstacles is maintained, then with a little imagination some challenging courses can be set up. However, it is important to stress the dangers to the children before commencing any activity. Establish a list of dos and don'ts and provide effective supervision – either by leading the group around the circuit and assisting them with potentially dangerous obstacles, or by having helpers posted at various locations. The list of dos and don'ts might be as follows.

1 Don't climb so high that you feel you can't climb down or jump off safely (establish a maximum height off the ground with the pupils, and practise jumping-off skills – keep knees bent, aim to land on two feet, jump on to a level surface, jump clear of protruding obstacles).

2 Keep clear of moving equipment.

3 Stop the equipment moving before attempting to get on or off.

4 Hold on to equipment with both hands.

5 Don't ignore safety rules or signs.

Assessment: by direct observation

Cross-curricular links: Environment; Health and Fitness; ICT; Language

Pupil resources: none

Extension and Enrichment: find out where the nearest Adventure Playground is to your home

Vocabulary: spotting, rules, signs, assault

Gymnasium confidence course

JUMP

TABLE

STEPS

TRAMPET

CRASH MAT

INCLINED LADDER

TRAVERSE WALL BARS

TOUCHING COLOURED TAPE

FOLLOW QUOIT TRAIL

BOXES FOR STEPPING STONES

CLIMB ON TO HORSE

CLIMB ROPE LADDER TO HALF HEIGHT DESCEND OTHER SIDE

ROPE SWING

BENCH WALK

BOX TRAVERSE

HOOP TUNNEL

BENCH WALK

Using adventure playgrounds

ropeway or zip wire

ropeswing

totem poles

climbing nets

pipes and tunnels

stepped
posts or boxes for climbing

fallen trees or fences for
scrambling

ditches for jumping across or
crossing on balancing logs

ropes suspended over
water or ditch

Walks and rambles (journeys into the countryside)

KS: 2/3

PoS: KS2: a, c; KS3: a, c, d

Aim: to provide the opportunity to plan and prepare for a journey; to experience a journey through an unfamiliar area of countryside; to increase conservation awareness and an awareness of the nature of country life; to develop navigational skills with Ordnance Survey (O.S.) maps

Time required: several theory-based classroom sessions of 30–50 minutes followed by a journey of between 3 and 8 hours

Location: low-level land (below 600 m above sea-level and not wilderness such as high mountain or moorland), open countryside, coastal (for example, South Downs Way), waymarked trails, forestry/country park trails, town pocket parks, national parks, national nature reserves, Sites of Special Scientific Interest (SSSI), Areas of Outstanding Natural Beauty (AONB)

Resources: 1:50,000 O.S. maps of area (preferably laminated or contained in a clear plastic map case/plastic bag), leader's kit (see 'Planning a visit', pages 81–5)

Target group: 11–13-year-olds (shorter, less demanding walks for the younger ones); See 'Planning a visit' for suggested pupil/staff ratios

Teacher's guidance notes

A journey into an unfamiliar, stimulating environment is deemed to be a desirable aspect of the KS2/3 OAA PoS. To be successful, the journey requires careful planning and a well-defined purpose that the pupils are aware of.

For practical reasons, the journey will be best undertaken on foot. Other journeys on water – using canoes, for example – may be possible with small groups after further training; alternatively, larger vessels and qualified staff may be sought for journeys with larger groups (for example, a fleet of longboats could stimulate cross-curricular links with History by investigating the origins of the longboat, Viking voyages, etc.).

Trips in winter conditions require extra precautions, although they do have the benefit of providing opportunities to see changes in vegetation.

The journey can provide a means of exploring a new environment, providing the pupils with a sense of discovery and an awareness of man's heritage of exploration and discovery (a well-documented aspect of our evolution which again could initiate a cross-curricular link with History – for example, Scott of the Antarctic). The journey also provides an opportunity to learn about the environment in which the activity is taking place (for example, coniferous forest plantations, fauna and flora,

topography and physical relief, erosion, pollution, conservation of natural habitats). Preliminary training in the country code and in hill, coastal and seashore safety (if applicable) will instil a disciplined, respectful approach to the landscape ventured into.

1 Preliminary planning:

a see pages 81–5 on planning a visit

b determine the aims of the journey and the cross-curricular input that is required, if any (for example, Food Technology – nutritional needs; Geography – the work of rivers)

c pupil training through the supplied resources in:

○ walking skills and country code

○ basic map reading skills (pupils will gain more from the journey if they can relate the map to their own position, and small groups can take turns to lead the party)

○ climatic effects on the body (wet, cold, heat, sun)

KS2/3

○ clothing and personal equipment

○ elementary route planning

○ other safety considerations appropriate to the activity.

2 Other considerations:

○ prevailing weather – a shorter, less demand-ing alternative route should be devised for bad weather

○ length of the journey – 2–5 miles plus pos-sibly a total of 300–400 metres of climbing should be considered

○ choice of venue – is it stimulating, will it fit the needs of the trip, how long will it take to transport the group to the start point, is overnight accommodation required?

○ how much time is required for the walk? – *see* pages 81–5

○ group size – large groups will be slow, more difficult to control and harder to keep together, so more staff will be required

○ cliff-top walks must be monitored more closely, especially in wet or windy weather – *see* pages 81–5.

3 Leader training and qualifications:

There are three qualifications available in Great Britain for supervising walking parties: the MLTB Mountain Leader Scheme (ML), the MLTB Walking Group Leader (WGL) and the CCPR Basic Expedition Leaders Award (BELA) (see page 95 for addresses). The former two are aimed principally at those whose aspirations lie in leading groups over high moorland or moun-tainous 'wilderness' areas. They require a big commitment, it is time consuming and therefore not really appropriate for this type of activity. The BELA award is closer to the mark and requires from the leader common sense, good map reading and first aid and emergency skills (see pages 81–5).

I would, however, suggest that a formal First Aid qualification, administered, for example, by the St. John/St. Andrew/Red Cross organisa-tions be obtained (*see* page 95).

Assessment: by direct observation, worksheets

Cross-curricular links: Environment; Science; Technology; History; Geography; ICT; Health and Safety

Pupil resources: none (It has not been practicable to reproduce detailed information on map work as this is widely available in Geography textbooks.)

Extension and Enrichment:

1 Take a road atlas and try to locate two long distance footpaths (e.g. The South Downs Way). Draw the routes on your map

2 Using ICT try to locate two areas of outstanding natural beauty (AONB) and add them to your map

Vocabulary: rambling, national park, AONB, scenic heritage, reserve, country park, forestry commission, public right of way (PROW), country code

Journeys into the countryside

A journey into the countryside can be very enjoyable, especially if you live in a town or city. You will get the chance to see just how beautiful natural areas can be, and possibly see wildlife in its natural surroundings. You may be lucky enough to visit a National Park.

A National Park is an area of land that has been recognised as being of outstanding natural beauty with spectacular natural formations such as waterfalls, lakes and mountains. There are special rules regarding the use of the land to make sure that it does not get spoiled. We call this type of protection **conservation**.

Look at the map below. How many National Parks are there in England and Wales? Find out which one is nearest to where you live – mark your home on the map. Also, find out about Scotland's Scenic Heritage Areas. What are Ireland's special areas known as?

**NATIONAL PARKS OF
ENGLAND AND WALES**

////// National Parks

Northumberland

Lake District

North York Moors

Yorkshire
Dales

Peak District

Snowdonia

Broads

Pembrokeshire
Coast

Brecon
Beacons

New
Forest

Exmoor

Dartmoor

| 0 | 25 | 50 | miles |
| 0 | 50 | 100 | kilometres |

The Country Code

You may visit a Country Park (a sort of mini National Park), or a forest, or follow the route of a way-marked trail. All land in this country – even the National Parks – is privately owned, some by the National Trust (a charity which purchases areas of land for the public to use), and some by the Forestry Commission (which provides trails for visitors to follow through the forest and for people who work on the land such as farmers).

Whenever we go on to private land we should make sure that we are following a Public Right of Way. This might be a footpath, a bridleway (for horses and cycles as well) or a byway. All of these are shown on the maps you will be using.

If you are visiting the area for the first time, then your journey becomes more of an exploration into the unknown, like the journeys made by famous explorers such as Scott of the Antarctic. Can you think of any more?

On a separate piece of paper, draw a picture to illustrate each of the points in the Country Code. These are listed below.

- Go carefully on country roads
- Respect the life of the countryside
- Tread lightly to reduce footpath erosion
- Don't pick flowers; take a photograph or make a drawing instead
- Don't climb over and damage stone walls or fences
- Fasten all gates
- Keep dogs under control
- Keep to paths across farmland
- Don't leave litter
- Don't contaminate water supplies
- Protect wildlife, plants and trees

Effects of cold, heat, rain, snow and wind

KS: 2/3

PoS: KS2: a, c; KS3: a, c, d

Aim: to show pupils how the elements can threaten one's well-being; to emphasise the need for a conservation-minded attitude to life; to reduce pollution and halt ozone depletion

Time required: three sessions of 30–50 minutes

Location: classroom and school playing fields

Resources: two mercury thermometers per group, colouring pencils and paper, pens

Target group: 11–13-year-olds. A class of 30, divided into groups of four for windchill experiment no. 2

KS2/3

Teacher's guidance notes

Ideally this information is best delivered as part of a preparation programme for a journey into the countryside. A knowledge of the effects of climatic conditions on the body is most important for anybody who ventures out of doors to pursue challenging activities. By learning how to keep warm and dry in bad weather, or cool and free from the harmful effects of the sun in hot weather, the pupil will not only be able to enjoy activities more but will also be less likely to fall ill.

If any of the wind-chill experiments are undertaken, make sure that you choose a windy day and contrasting locations for the thermometer experiments.

The colouring exercise and instructional diagram graphics task will hopefully reinforce any teacher-led examination of the photocopiable material.

In looking at this section we can introduce the concept of conservation and increase environmental awareness by illustrating how man is destroying the planet through over-indulgence and exploitation. The issues of deforestation, the build-up of greenhouse gases and ozone layer depletion can be easily linked to this area of study. This in turn can lead into discussions on conservation measures such as planting more trees and grasslands, using smaller cars and unleaded fuel, sharing transport, using ozone-friendly products, and finding out about conservation bodies such as Greenpeace, Friends of the Earth, the Countryside Agency and the National Trust.

Assessment: by examination of pupils' classwork and experiment results

Cross-curricular links: Environment; Health and Fitness; ICT; Health and Safety

Pupil resources: see worksheets

Extension and Enrichment:

1 Make a list of things you can do to help conserve the environment

2 Look on the internet or library for names of organisations associated with conservation

Vocabulary: conservation, wind chill, exposure, bivouac, ozone, CFC, greenhouse effect, lapse rate, summit

Bad weather and the cold

Name _____

If you get ...

COLD

WET

TIRED

... you could develop ...

EXPOSURE

... and collapse through ...

POOR CLOTHING

INADEQUATE FOOD

INJURY OR FATIGUE

... in which case ...

1 Stop and rest

2 Put on spare clothing

3 Eat sugary foods and make hot drinks

4 Shelter from wind and rain. Climb into a bivouac bag. Find an old building or a wall. Erect a tent or make a shelter if you can

5 Try to summon help with distress signals. If possible, send two fit persons to dial 999

Draw a set of pictures to illustrate your actions to deal with exposure.

Hot weather and the sun

Too much sun can cause you to collapse with fatigue and dehydration

The emissions from car exhaust pipes, smoke and the cutting down of trees in the equatorial rain forests is creating what is known as the 'Greenhouse Effect'. More and more carbon dioxide in the atmosphere is causing the planet to heat up.

How can we reduce the Greenhouse Effect?

Prevention of heat disorders in hot weather

1   Keep fit

2   Conserve energy; don't overdo it

3   Drink and rest at regular intervals

4   Keep out of the sun as much as possible

5   Good quality food of a high nutritional value can help

6   Wear loose, well-ventilated clothing, sunglasses and a sun hat

7   The ozone layer protects us from harmful UVA rays from the sun. The ozone layer has been reduced by CFCs from aerosol cans. You can help to preserve the ozone layer by using ozone friendly products

8   To protect us from UVB rays (which can cause sunburn) and UVA rays (which can cause skin cancers and cataracts of the eye), we must use a suncream. The higher the factor number, the greater the level of protection

Label this drawing with the numbers of the points listed above. If you have time, use colours to show each point more clearly.

The next time you go shopping, try to find out what is the highest factor suncream on the supermarket shelves.

Wind chill

When the speed of air increases, its pressure decreases; this in turn causes cooling. Strong winds will have a marked effect on the temperature in exposed locations, for example a mountain ridge.

Try these other wind chill experiments.

1 Assess the windproofing of your clothing by blowing through the garment. Can you feel the air coming through the other side?

Now choose a windy spot on the school field. Put your best windproof garment on, then take it off again after a few minutes. Notice any differences?

2 **Equipment required**: two mercury thermometers. Choose a windy day to measure the temperature on the school field in the following locations:

a the centre spot of the field (a = ?°C);

b the edge of the field bounded by a wall or fence and so protected from the wind (b = ?°C).

Note the difference between the two temperatures and determine the wind chill factor:

$$\text{WIND CHILL FACTOR} = \frac{b - a}{b} \times 100\%$$

The lapse rate

In general, as you increase your height above sea level (for example, climbing a mountain), the temperature will decrease by about 3°C per 300m. Therefore, if the valley temperature was 3°C and you were going to climb a 300 m hill, the temperature at the summit would be at freezing point. On a windy day, the summit temperature will probably be lower still! Rain in the valley may be falling as snow on the summit.

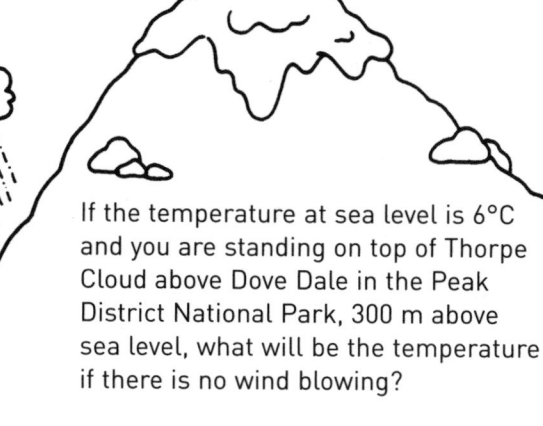

If the temperature at sea level is 6°C and you are standing on top of Thorpe Cloud above Dove Dale in the Peak District National Park, 300 m above sea level, what will be the temperature if there is no wind blowing?

Electrical storms

KS: 2/3

PoS: KS2: a, c; KS3: a, c, d

Aim: to educate pupils in how to minimise the risk of being struck by lightning during thunderstorms

Time required: 20–25 minutes

Location: classroom

Resources: pens

Target group: 11-13-year-olds, a class of 30

Teacher's guidance notes

A useful learning exercise which can be completed in class as an academic exercise. Explain that very few people get struck by lightning.

Once again, this work may be included in the preparation for a journey into the countryside. However, it is a good idea for children to know what to do if caught in a storm as a matter of course. Also, by learning a little about how lightning and thunder are formed we may help to reduce the fear associated with these awesome natural phenomena.

Pupils are required to digest the text and to relate the information given to the graphics. Pose the question: 'What is an electrical storm?' Try to lead pupils into realising that lightning is a powerful surge of electricity created by hot and cold air currents clashing and generating an electrical charge. The lightning conducts its way to the earth by 'hopping a ride' on droplets of rain (as water conducts electricity). It looks for the easiest way to earth via tall buildings, etc. Further discussion could lead to the need to 'earth' electrical appliances to prevent discharge through

your body, electrical conductors on tall buildings and the need to insulate with rubber and plastic. Perhaps you could explain the dangers of using electrical equipment near water, such as in the bath or outside when it is raining.

Explain that thunder is the sound of the electricity rushing through the air, rather like a supersonic jet crashing through the sound barrier. You could also explain why you see the flash of lightning several seconds before the clap of thunder – i.e. because of the different speeds of light and sound. A useful follow-up activity is to take the group out on to the school fields and position a pupil at the furthest point possible from the rest of the group with a pair of cymbals. Get him to hold them up and crash them together once; there will be a delay before the sound reaches you.

Finally, explain that if you are with someone who gets struck by lightning they will probably need resuscitating and treating for severe burns. This could lead the group nicely into the activity on page 51 (Emergency Action).

Assessment: examination of pupils' answers on the worksheet

Cross-curricular links: Science; Health and Safety

Pupil resources: *see* worksheet

Extension and Enrichment: draw a diagram to show how an electrical storm develops in the atmosphere

Vocabulary: electrical charge, discharge, conduct, ridge, earth

Electrical storms

Name _____

Electrical storms can be dangerous; they can kill. Lightning is attracted to high and prominent ground such as mountains, trees and towers.

○ If you are on an exposed ridge, carefully move off to a lower terrain

○ On no account shelter from the storm under trees, by walls or in rock cavities and land projections

○ Try to find some dry rocks on a shallow slope at the base of a hollow

○ Insulate yourself by standing or sitting on a survival bag, rope or rucksack. Avoid bodily contact with the ground – crouch or sit with the feet brought up to the chest

○ Wet ropes will act like electrical wires because the water will conduct the electricity

○ Early warning signs of an approaching storm: hair raising as a result of static electricity; metal objects humming; rumbling noises in the distance

Look at the points above. Draw a lightning symbol ⚡ at each place on the illustration below where you would expect lightning ⚡ to strike. Put a circle around the correct place to be.

Remember, lightning will always try to find the easiest, shortest route to earth.

Rivers

KS: 2/3

PoS: KS2: a, c; KS3: a, c, d

Aim: to increase the pupils' awareness of the dangers of moving water and to demonstrate safe methods of crossing

Time required: 30–50 minutes

Location: school playing fields for training, followed up with an actual crossing while on a journey*

Resources: stepping stones, tree stumps or upturned containers capable of withstanding the weight of a pupil, flags or pegs to mark the course of the river, measuring tape

Target group: 11–13-year-olds; a class of 30 in groups of 3, 6 and 1

KS2/3

Teacher's guidance notes

As before, this activity could form part of a preparation programme for a journey into the countryside. Emphasise that crossing any river is a risky business and should only be undertaken under the supervision of your teachers. These techniques should only be practised in very shallow water – perhaps up to knee height – where there is no danger of being swept away by the current. For deeper, fast flowing water a safety rope is needed. In such cases the crossing should only be carried out as an emergency procedure when no other alternative is available, not as an activity in its own right. *See* pages 86–91 for more information.

Practise the techniques shown on the school playing fields, using cones or flag markers to describe the route of an imaginary river. Indicate the direction of flow, the position of a weir, an overhanging tree, and rocks in the middle of the stream creating eddies. Design a river that includes a large bend, a shallow and a narrowing. The pupils will have to decide which is the safest place to cross.

Further 'downstream' you can arrange a line of stepping stones across the river and explain that the pupils must recross the river using the stones. Anyone 'falling in' has to start again. Make sure that the stones are not too far apart for the pupils.

Demonstrate how easy it is to knock someone over if they are facing downstream by pushing a basketball into the back of a pupil's knee (but take care!).

If during an off-site visit the opportunity to do a river crossing does present itself, then it is well worth doing. Always make a crossing yourself first to ascertain the suitability of the water (on a safety rope if you are in any doubt as to the strength of flow and depth).

Assessment: examination of the pupils' answers on the worksheet and observation in the field

Cross-curricular links: Geography; ICT; Health and Safety; Language

Pupil resources: *see* worksheet

Extension and Enrichment: moving water is also known as 'whitewater'. Some sports and activities make use of whitewater. Find out about as many as you can.

Vocabulary: flow, current, weir, eddy, upstream, downstream, flood

Rivers

Name _____

We may be required to cross a river on our journeys into the countryside. Rivers in upland areas often run fast and can be very dangerous in times of heavy rainfall. Only cross rivers in flood if there is no other alternative, and only then with a safety rope. Your teacher will know how to do this if it becomes necessary.

○ When do we cross? No bridge; long detour to bridge; darkness coming soon

○ Where do we cross? Current slowest; even bottom; shallow; no obstructions (e.g. overhanging trees); after a bend in the river; stepping stones

○ Where shouldn't we cross? Above waterfalls or weirs; bends; deep water; uneven bottom; in front of obstructions

Put a tick where you feel it is safe and a cross where it is not safe to cross:

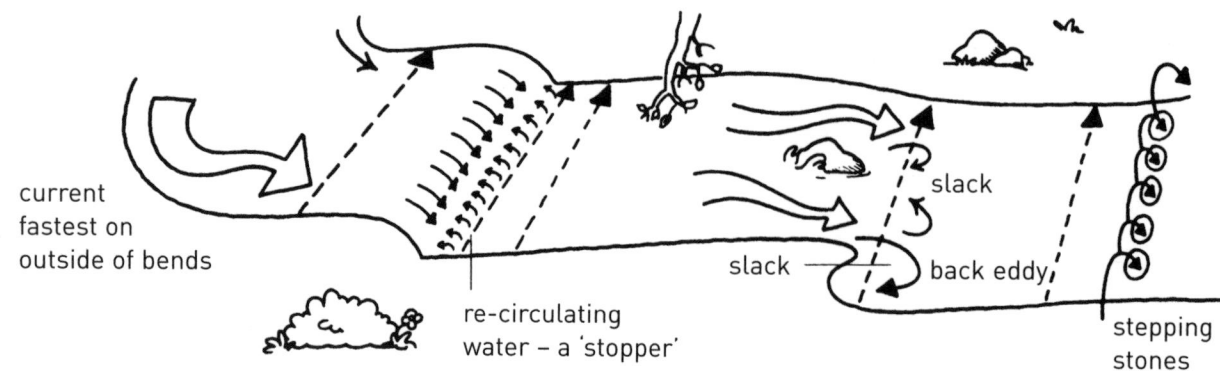

current fastest on outside of bends

re-circulating water – a 'stopper'

slack

slack — back eddy

stepping stones

○ Precautions: slacken rucksack straps; take off socks; roll up or take off trousers; always face upstream and ferry glide across

○ Stepping stones: stay balanced; wet rocks are slippery; look ahead

○ Crossing methods (only to be attempted in shallow water):

Three persons linking arms

One person with stick for support. Practise crossing stepping stones and these techniques in your school field.

'A' moves one space, then 'B', then 'C', then 'D', etc.

Always try to cross diagonally downstream.

Perhaps your teacher may find a place where you can practise these methods

Emergency action

KS: 2/3

PoS: KS2: a, c; KS3: a, c, d

Aim: to acquire a knowledge of life-saving skills and of how to deal with an emergency

Time required: approximately two sessions of 50 minutes

Location: classroom

Resources: 'Resuscitation Annie', triangular bandages, softwood splints (150 mm + 10 mm + 500 mm), a selection of plasters, sterile dressings

Target group: 11–13-year-olds. A class of 30 in groups of two

Teacher's guidance notes

One might argue that this core of knowledge and skill acquisition is the most important to learn in life, and yet how often is such training left to chance or completely ignored?

The best teaching strategies involve examination of the material in stages, interspersed with demonstrations by the teacher leading the activity and immediately followed by pupil participation. On no account let any pupil blow into the mouth of another when practising mouth-to-mouth resuscitation – demonstrate how to blow over the other side of the face. Points to emphasise are neck extension, loosening restrictive clothing, looking in the mouth for obstructions, looking for the rise and fall of the chest, action for vomiting, rate of inflation and recovery position. Resuscitation dolls are useful for practising cardiac compressions – **never let pupils practise this procedure on one another** as you can actually cause a cardiac arrest in this way.

It can be useful to contact the local First Aid organisation, which will be only too pleased to help you with any prograrnme of First Aid you may be planning. The supervising teacher should hold a valid First Aid certificate themselves for legal purposes. Resuscitation dolls may be loaned out from the First Aid organisations; the PE adviser should also be able to help in this area.

Contact the Royal Life Saving Society (RLSS) for the crib cards; they are free of charge. I feel that every child should possess one.

Points to note with the shoulder sling are that the fingers should protrude and that the knot (a reef knot) should be at the shoulder. For leg splints, look for bandages placed either side of the site of the fracture.

Assessment: by direct observation, questioning, feedback

Cross-curricular links: Health and Fitness; Citizenship; ICT; Health and Safety

Pupil resources: *see* worksheets

Extension and Enrichment:

1 How many different organisations do you know of that provide training in First Aid?

2 Produce a fact sheet on either the Mountain Rescue Services, Cave Rescue, Coastguard or Royal National Lifeboat Association

Vocabulary: resuscitation, immobilisation, conservation, fall line, fracture, international distress code, heat exhaustion, moorland, compound, wound, splint, casualty, signal, survival bag, bog, layering, shell, breathable, Ordnance Survey, terrain

Emergency action – First Aid

Everybody should know how to deal with emergencies. You may be able to save somebody's life, possibly that of a friend or relative.

○ Remove the victim from immediate danger if necessary. Summon help if required by using Distress Signals or dialling 999.

○ Carry out any First Aid that is required in the following order of priority: AIRWAY, BREATHING, CIRCULATION (ABC); bleeding, fractures, shock, other injuries.

○ Study the Royal Life Saving Society Emergency First Aid Card that your teacher has given you. Split up into pairs and have a go after your teacher has gone through the technique with you. **It is very important that you do not actually blow into your partner's mouth (blow over the far side of their head) or try to push down on their chest**. To be safe, you should practise on a dummy (a 'resuscitation Annie').

○ Bleeding from cuts or wounds: remove any foreign bodies (glass, stones, etc.) and clean the wound with water or antiseptic. In the case of large wounds, slow down the flow of blood by pressing down with a pad (a sterile dressing) and bandaging firmly. Get medical help as soon as possible. With small wounds, clean as above, then apply a small plaster.

○ Fractures, sprains and strains: do not move anyone who complains of neck or back pain, or of loss of feeling. Injuries to the arms can be immobilised with a sling (e.g. a triangular bandage).

○ Injuries to the leg can be immobilised using a splint (e.g. a piece of wood) and bandages (not directly over the fracture). A sprained ankle may just need a cold compress to reduce swelling, and then bandaging.

Get medical help as soon as possible

Now try to make an arm sling and leg splint for your partner; then swap roles.

○ Shock: anyone who has had an accident will be in shock. They will complain of feeling sick and faint. Lay them down before they fall down! Reassure them and keep them warm. **Do not give any accident victim anything to eat or drink**.

○ Burns: immerse in cold water, cover with a wet cloth and seek help.

○ Insect stings: pluck out any barb that may be protruding, apply insect bite cream if you have any to hand, and seek help.

○ Dog bites: clean the wound, stop any bleeding and seek help.

○ Snake bites: the only poisonous snake in Britain is the adder. It has a V-shaped pattern on its head. It will only bite if threatened. If someone is bitten, try to wash out the venom with water and get the victim to medical help as soon as possible. The poison can be life-threatening in some cases.

○ Protect all casualties by keeping them warm, dry and sheltered from the wind. If possible put spare, dry clothing on the victim before placing them in a sleeping bag (if available) and bivouac bag. Extra protection can be gained by placing the legs into a rucksack. **Remember: do not give drinks or food to anyone who is suffering from internal injuries or who may require an operation**.

○ Reassure the victim if they are conscious. **Remember: do not attempt to move casualties suffering from neck or back injuries**.

The journey into the countryside (1)

Name _____

What should I do if I get lost or separated from the rest of the group? Stay in one place and try to attract attention by:

○ Using the International Alpine Rescue Code (six shouts, whistles or torch flashes per minute followed by a minute's pause – a rescue party will acknowledge with three per minute)

○ Shouting! Some of your class will be very good at this!

○ Waving an orange or red article in the air (e.g. a plastic survival bag)

Plastic Survival Bag
Could also be used to
shelter from wind and rain

Put your spare clothing on and try to keep warm. Shelter from the wind and rain. Tuck into your emergency food. Keep signalling for help.

Can you think of another distress signal? Make a drawing of your answer in the space below.

What are the hazards I should be prepared for?

○ Electrical storms

○ Rivers

○ Cold, wet, windy weather

○ Exposure

○ Wind chill

○ Hot, dry weather and heat exhaustion

The journey into the countryside (2)

Name _____

What should we wear for our journey into the countryside?

On our feet? A pair of training shoes or Wellington boots is a good idea, especially if they have a good tread pattern and ankle support (it is very easy to twist your ankle on rough country paths). However, if you have a pair of fabric or leather walking boots, then this would be even better.

Does your footwear have:

a good tread?

ankle support?

strong laces?

Leather boots can be waterproofed to some extent by rubbing a waterproof compound (available from outdoor shops) into the leather. Sprays can be bought for fabric boots.

Beware of new boots: they can be very painful and create blisters very quickly. Blisters are no joke when you are on a walk! Wear your boots around town for a few weeks and find out where the sore points are. If you start to feel your boots rubbing, stop and tighten the laces before a blister develops. If your feet start to feel sore, stop and put a plaster on the area of discomfort. If you do develop a blister, make the plaster into a ring pad to relieve the pressure. Do not prick blisters.

make a ring-pad for blisters

cover with second plaster

Alternatively, you can use one of the many specialised 'blister' plasters now available.

The journey into the countryside (3)

Name _____

What should we wear on our bodies?

We have to be prepared for bad weather. This means trying to keep dry and warm by wearing clothing that will keep out the wind, rain and snow and insulate us from the cold. In hot, fine weather we will want to stay cool.

The outer shell. We can keep the wind, rain and snow out by wearing an outer layer known as a 'shell'. A jacket that has a 'proofing' is required; the proofing makes the jacket waterproof.

We may get wet inside from sweat trapped inside the shell when we are working hard – walking uphill, for instance – but this is much better than getting chilled by an icy blast of wind or saturated by a downpour! Really keen outdoor adventurists wear waterproofs that can 'breathe'. However, these are very expensive and not necessary for our ventures.

Things to look for in waterproofs:

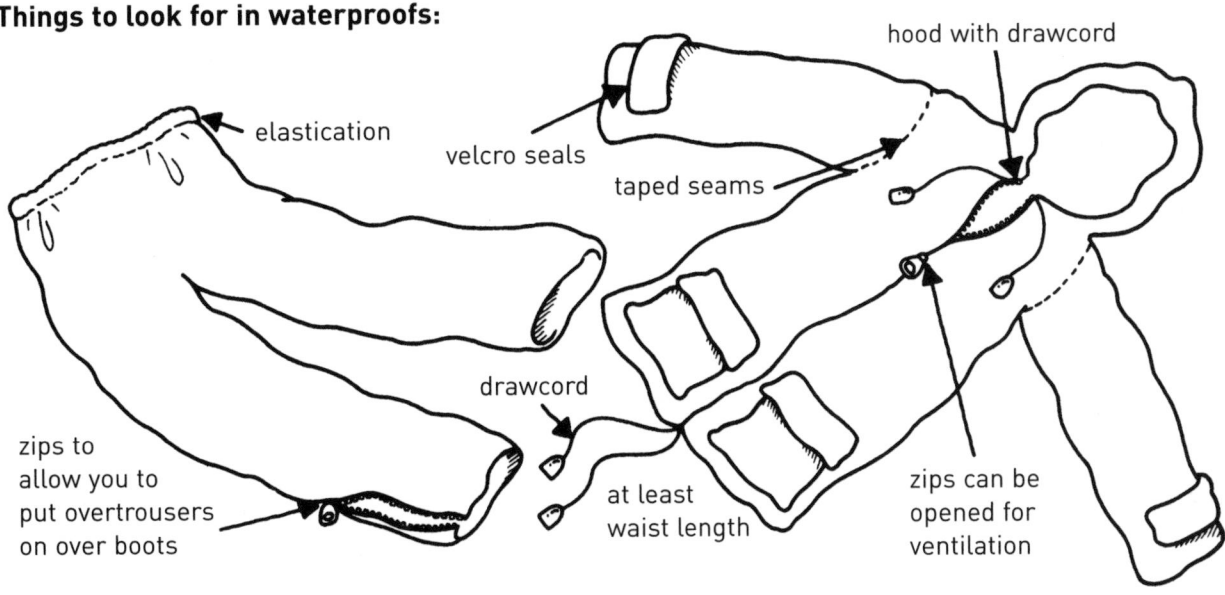

How many of these features do your waterproofs have?

Waterproof trousers are useful for the legs as well, but don't worry too much about this. It is your upper body that needs the most protection to prevent you from becoming a victim of exposure.

Tracksuit trousers, jogging bottoms or a pair of trousers that dry out quickly when wet and are reasonably windproof (remember the wind chill experiments?) are sufficient protection for your legs. In cold weather you could wear some pyjama bottoms underneath for added warmth, or you may own some long johns.

In summer, a pair of shorts can be worn underneath your trousers. Avoid jeans if you can – they offer no warmth when wet and take a very long time to dry out.

The journey into the countryside (4)

Name _____

Inside the 'shell'

The shell only needs to be worn in wet, windy conditions. Inside the shell we need to have a number of layers so that we can regulate our body temperatures according to how hard we are working and how much heat we are generating. This is how the layers work:

Where is the most heat escaping?

Several thin layers will be more flexible and warmer than one thick one. Here is a suggested 'layering' set-up for your walk:

extra layers for winter

In winter you should increase your layers. The best layering materials are fleecy sweaters and jackets or woollens. These garments are very warm for their weight (even when wet!) and dry out very quickly. Ski anoraks (which are normally windproof), sweat shirts, rugby shirts and T-shirts can all be used for our walk.

What about my head, feet and hands? These areas of your body lose heat more quickly than anywhere else. On all walks it is wise to have a pair of gloves and a ski-style hat or balaclava. A scarf may also be useful. Wear a pair of thick socks if you have them; failing that a pair of football socks and a pair of thin socks may be the answer. Try to keep your feet dry; wet, cold feet are very unpleasant. In summer, it will be necessary to protect your head from the sun with a baseball cap or some other form of sun hat.

On a separate piece of paper, make up checklists for clothing required on journeys from April to October, and from November to March.

The journey into the countryside (5)

Name _____

What else should we take with us?

○ A spare layer such as a ski anorak, fleece jacket, sweat shirt or sweater for rest stops and emergencies

○ A packed lunch (sandwiches, crisps, chocolate bar, nuts and raisins, biscuits, apple, orange). Food should be convenient to carry and have a high carbohydrate content (e.g. sugar) for energy

○ A sugar-based drink for energy. Hot drinks in vacuum flasks will be welcome in wintry weather. Cans of fizzy drink are not really suitable – drink little and often is the best policy, and once you open a can you have to drink all of it! Keeping fluid levels up is very important; you must replace fluid lost by sweating in order to prevent dehydration

○ Food for emergencies (not to be taken unless your teacher tells you to or you are desperate!). This could be a king-sized bar of chocolate, or Kendal mint cake which can be bought from any outdoor shop

○ A reliable torch, spare batteries and a spare bulb in case our walk finishes in the dark. Walking in the dark can be very exciting!

○ A whistle to attract attention if you get lost, but please no whistling as we go along. We are here to enjoy the peace and quiet

○ A small, personal First Aid kit

○ Your teacher will provide each group with an Ordnance Survey map of the area and possibly a plastic survival bag if the route takes you on to high ground

○ A small rucksack, big enough to hold all the items you need to carry. Make sure that you either wrap up all the items you need to carry in plastic bags or line the sack with a large plastic bag (e.g. a dustbin liner)

See if you can identify and label the items above in the drawings below. (On some walks your teacher may decide that some of these items are not needed.)

YOU PROVIDE

TEACHER PROVIDES

The journey into the countryside (6)

Name _____

What other skills do I need to learn?

Complete the information below by making your own 'cartoon' drawings on a separate piece of paper to illustrate the points more clearly.

A Types of terrain

1 Grassy slopes. Nice to walk on because the grass has a cushioning effect, but – 'Whoops!' – they can be very slippery when wet!

2 Heather moorland. Heather is a shrub-like plant. Tread carefully.

3 Peat bogs – 'Yuk!'. Messy and tiring to trek through.

4 Scree. These are slopes of pebbles and larger stones which are very tiring to climb but can be exciting to descend (don't go too fast). Dig your heels in and don't lean forwards. Bend your knees as in skiing.

5 Rough, rocky paths can cause you to stumble and fall. They have been formed by the thousands of pairs of feet that have tramped over them, eroding the topsoil. Footpath erosion is a conservation problem in some areas such as the National Parks. Wardens and volunteers are constantly carrying out restoration work – like the roadworks on the motorways! If the path is steep, use your hands to support yourself. Remember that the rock itself can vary in texture from smooth sedimentary rock such as limestone, to coarse volcanic rock such as granite. (Your teacher may have a number of rock samples to show you in class.) Rocks are very slippery when wet.

B Walking skills

1 We must always keep together to prevent someone getting lost. We should go at the pace of the slowest. It is not a race: let's try to encourage those who may not be as athletic as others.

2 We must try to develop a steady, rhythmic pace. It is foolish to rush off at breakneck speed, because you will become tired very quickly. On steep slopes, you will have to shorten your stride, walk at a slower pace than normal, and rest more often.

3 Have you ever noticed how most very steep paths and roads up mountains zig-zag up and down, or gradually climb at a lesser angle around the hillside? You will find that ascending and descending slopes in this way will be far less tiring than attacking the 'fall line' direct. Ask your teacher what is meant by the 'fall line'.

4 We will try to set ourselves targets to reach before we stop for a rest. See them as little challenges – places which offer a good view and shelter from wind and rain.

5 We will probably have one or two food stops to break up the journey and keep our energy levels up. Don't eat all of your lunch at the first stop!

6 Use your clothing wisely; put on extra layers when you stop for a break. Don't climb hills with excessive clothing on, because you will overheat and sweat rapidly.

7 Most accidents occur towards the end of a day, normally when descending. Try to concentrate and look where you are going at all times.

Journey into the countryside (7)

Name _____

1   We are going to observe one minute's silence when instructed to do so by your teacher. In the space below, write down every noise you hear.

How do these noises differ from noises in the town or city?

If you were able to do the same experiment in your town or city before you came on the journey, compare your two lists.

2   As you travel through the countryside on your journey, observe the following and write down any differences (numbers, type, size, shape, etc.) compared with similar features in the town or city.

a   Rivers and streams _____

b   Lakes _____

c   The shape of the land ('topography') _____

d   Vegetation on the ground _____

e   Trees _____

f   Soil _____

g   Animals and birds _____

h   Flowers _____

i   Fences and walls _____

j   Houses/dwellings _____

k   Paths _____

l   Motor vehicles _____

m People _____

n   Roads _____

Ask your teacher if you do not understand any of these questions.

Orienteering (advanced)

KS: 2/3

PoS: KS2: a, b, c; KS3: a, b, c

Aim: to develop problem-solving abilities through navigational activities; to introduce the sport of orienteering; to help pupils work together, taking turns leading, being led and sharing thoughts

Time required: 30–50 minutes, or up to half a day on off-site courses

Location: school grounds, permanent offsite courses in country parks, Forestry Commission recreation areas

Resources: maps (waterproofed), pen/pencil, answer sheet, navigating compass, watch, whistle (for use if lost), markers (painted or pinned). Large-scale maps of your school and surrounding areas may be obtained from the education department of the O.S. or local planning office

Target group: 11–13-year-olds

Teacher's guidance notes

Orienteering is a relatively easy activity to implement, catering for large groups. It is also an excellent activity for getting pupils to work together in small groups, recording and evaluating, and exploring.

There is much that can be done on-site and in the local community – indeed, all the preparatory exercises included here do precisely that. Note that there is a great emphasis on the responsibility of team members to one another: for instance, in timed events it is the last member back who determines the team's final time. Children are encouraged not to split up during the course, and safety is emphasised in cases of potential contact with water or traffic. For off-site courses, safety is even more important since close supervision is very difficult. Basic road safety is essential for any course that brings the pupils into contact with traffic, as is a strategy for returning to base or summoning help.

Where possible, try to devise navigation games that require pupils to start at different locations or to find different markers.

Courses that require a staggered start can be difficult to manage and tedious for those waiting; they can also be unfair as the waiting groups have more time to study the map. Time does not have to feature prominently in these activities, except perhaps for a competition at the end of the course. Groups of four are ideal.

Assessment: by analysis of recordings and direct observation, questioning, feedback

Cross-curricular links: Health and Fitness; Geography; Environment; Citizenship

Pupil resources: *see* worksheets

Extension and Enrichment:

1 Where is the nearest 'permanent' Orienteering course to your home?

2 Using the internet find the website of the British Orienteering Federation (BOF). Gain information on competitions: when? where? who for? entry rules?

Vocabulary: orienteering, map, compass, markers, bearing protractor, control points, navigation, permanent course, orientation, setting the map, thumbing, aiming-off, scale, pacing, fight, magnetic

Orienteering (1)

Name _____

Orienteering is very much like a treasure hunt. It is a game that uses the skills of map reading to locate checkpoints within a certain area of land. Orienteering is an interesting way of getting out and about in the countryside.

Orienteering courses can be set up in any area; even built-up areas can be used to create a challenging course. Home-made, urban-based courses can make use of street maps, altered slightly to hide the names of selected public buildings and points of interest.

You must always be careful of traffic in built-up areas. Never cross the road without stopping and looking first. Always use the Green Cross Code. Always cross well away from bends, never between parked cars and, wherever possible, by pelican crossings, subways or central reservation islands.

Equipment for orienteering

1 A map of large scale with identifiable features and control points.

2 Outdoor games kit and tracksuit/jogging suit, hat and gloves for cold weather. Most people who do orienteering (called 'orienteers') tuck their trousers into long socks so that they don't flap around and get caught in brambles, etc.

Orienteering (2)

Name _____

Your teacher may be able to arrange a visit to an orienteering event or a permanent orienteering course. The venue will probably be a forest.

Permanent orienteering courses have been set up in lots of forests, heathlands, country parks and moorlands. Throughout the United Kingdom, most are supervised by the Forestry Commission or local authorities. Specially prepared maps are usually available from a warden's office or the offices of those directly responsible for the course.

Orienteering courses normally take the form of red and white painted posts or boards bearing an identification mark – if you are in a competition – or a piece of equipment designed to leave a symbol on your route card.

Competitive orienteering is a popular sport. Teams or individuals race against each other, hoping to find all the markers and complete the course in the shortest possible time. Failure to locate a marker incurs time penalty points which are added on to your finishing time.

There are many competitions organised throughout the country each year for all levels of ability. If you would like to find out more about the sport of orienteering, ask your teacher for the address of The British Orienteering Federation.

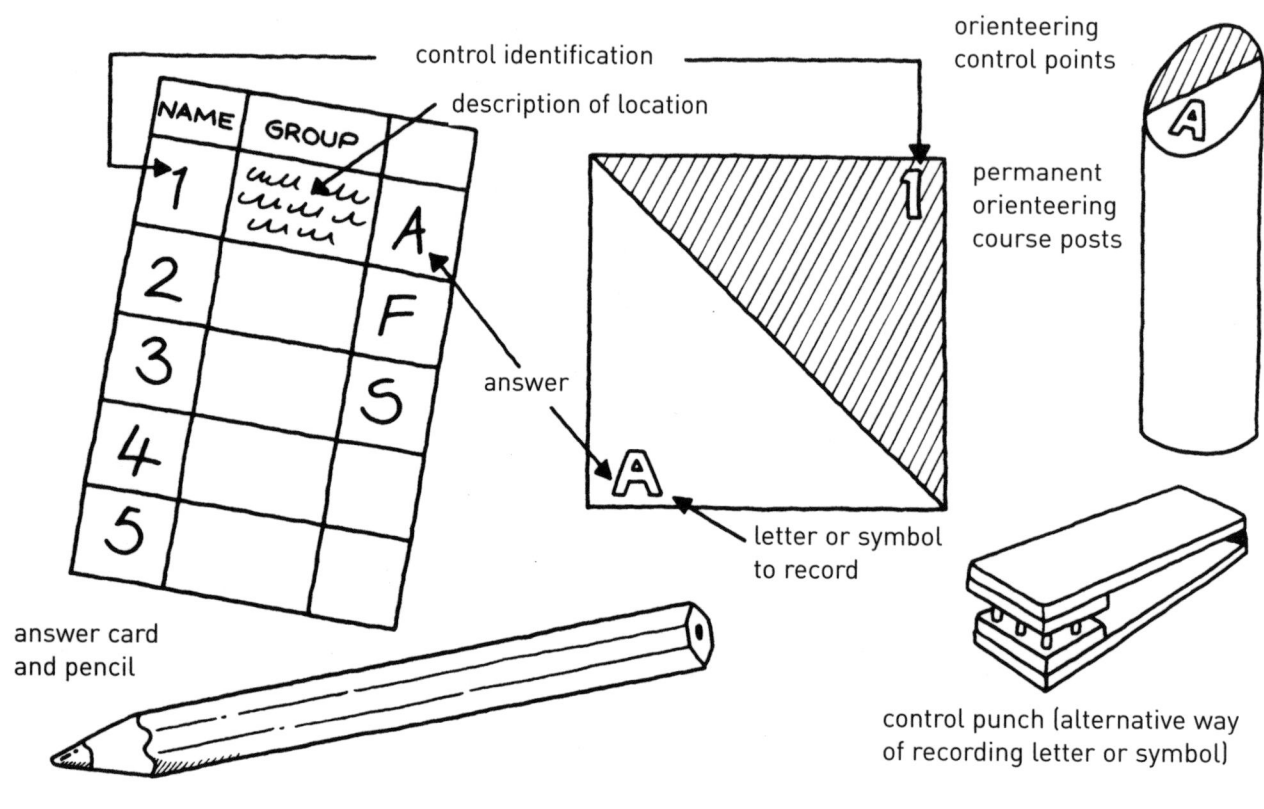

answer card and pencil

control identification

description of location

answer

letter or symbol to record

orienteering control points

permanent orienteering course posts

control punch (alternative way of recording letter or symbol)

Orienteering (3)

Name _____

The navigating compass

The model shown in the drawing below is the most common form of navigating compass used for orienteering and has all the features necessary for the compass navigation you will be doing with your teacher.

When carrying out any compass navigation techniques, always make sure that the RED (North) end of the compass needle aligns with the orienting arrow in the compass housing.

millimetre scale

50

40

30

20

10

base

bearing direction arrow

set/read bearing here

rotating protractor

orienting arrow

compass needle

orienting lines

liquid filled (damped) compass housing

Orienteering (4)

Name _____

Orienteering skills

Pacing techniques

Pacing can help you determine distances when moving around the course. The average person takes 60 double paces per 100 metres.

If the map scale is 1:10,000, then 1 cm = 10,000 cm = 100 m

2 cm

therefore
2 cm = 200 m

A
x

x
B

L   R   L

1 double pace

If 160 double paces are used (i.e. count one foot movement only) then the rate is 80 per 100 m.

On a steep slope, the orienteer finds that his pacing goes up to 120 per 100 m.
How many paces must he take when AB = 4 cm and the slope is steep?

Answer _____

An orienteer will work out his or her personal pacing for level, uphill and downhill terrain.

Exercise

Now try some pacing techniques on your school field.

a Select a known distance between two features in the field on fairly level ground. Count the number of double paces taken to cover this distance. Repeat this several times, walking back and forth to find the average. Work out the number of paces per 100 m. This is your personal pacing rate for level ground.

b Now repeat the experiment for a steep slope of known distance.

PERSONAL PACING RECORD

Name: _____

Pacing for level ground: _____

Pacing for steep slopes: _____

Orienteering (5)

Name _____

Orienteering skills

Setting the map
This technique will help you to decide which way to go. To set the map, draw imaginary lines from yourself to features on the map. Turn the map until your imaginary line points to the feature.

YOUR POSITION

Junctions

Always stop at junctions in paths and set your map to make sure that you know in which direction to continue.

Thumbing

This involves keeping your thumb on your present position. You will be able to save valuable minutes in this way every time you need to consult the map.

YOUR POSITION

Orienteering (6)

Name _____

Orienteering skills

Working out your route

Take note of the nature of the terrain between checkpoints. Avoid the 'fight' shown on the map below – it is always a fight to get through! Going in a straight line may not always be the quickest route.

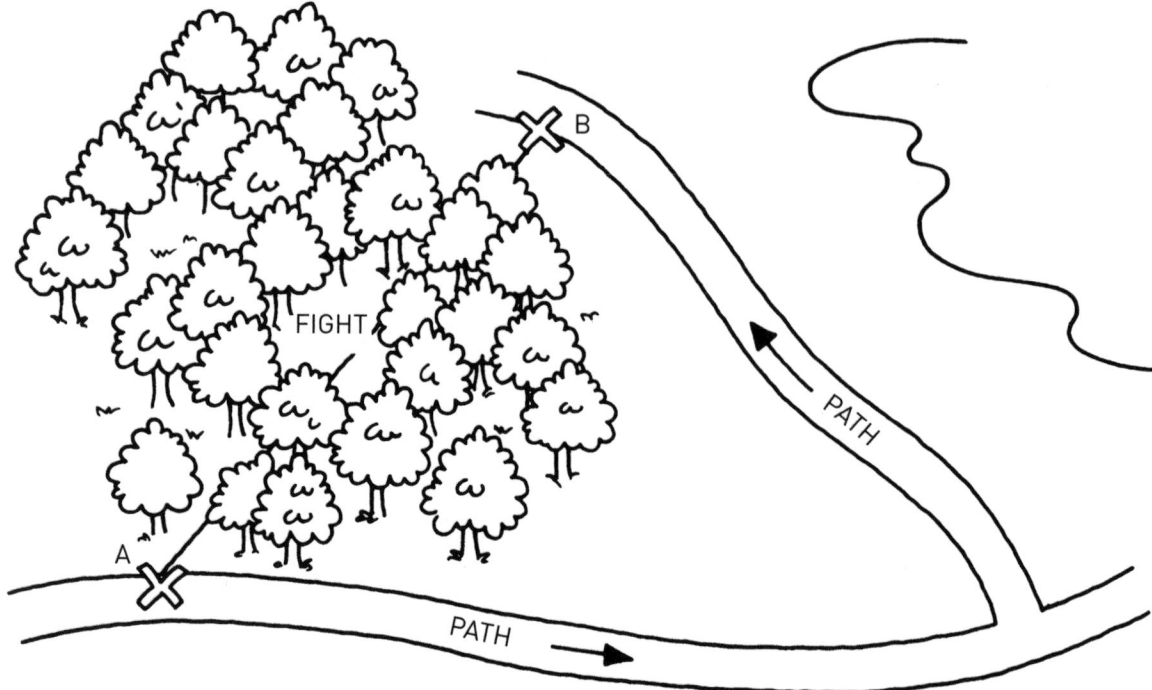

Exercise

Your teacher will provide you with an orienteering map of your school field or local area. Use the skills you now have to complete the course.

Notes

1 There will be a 10-minute penalty for each missed or incorrect answer

2 Stay together. Your group time is calculated on the last member of your group returning

3 Take extra care near any water

4 Don't climb bridges or go on to roads

5 Use paths

6 Use the Green Cross Code on routes in built-up areas

Orienteering (7)

Name _____

Compass techniques

To set a bearing of 20°:

a rotate protractor until 20° is at the top

b rotate yourself and the compass on the spot until the RED (North) end of the compass needle lines up with the 'N'. Look along the bearing direction arrow.

protractor

bearing direction arrow

Important – Keep away from metal objects because they will affect the magnetic needle. See what happens when you move your compass close to a chair or table with metal legs.

Exercise

Now go out on to your school field and take the bearings listed by your teacher at the specified locations (e.g. athletics shed – 40°). Write down the landmark you see on the bearing at each checkpoint.

GROUP NAMES: _____

LOCATION	BEARING	LANDMARK

Orienteering (8)

Name _____

Exercise

Go to the location specified by your teacher and take the first bearing listed. Walk the specified number of paces on this bearing and take the second bearing and so on until you have completed the course. Leave a coloured marker at each checkpoint.

Where have you ended up? Can you name the shape formed by your markers?

Collect them up and move on to the next station when your teacher tells you to. Move clockwise around the course.

Walk _ _ _ _ paces on each bearing.

LOCATION 1: 3 markers

Bearings:
120°
270°
 60°
Shape? _ _ _ _ _ _ _ _ _ _ _ _ _ _ _ _

LOCATION 2: 4 markers

Bearings:
 90°
180°
270°
360°
Shape? _ _ _ _ _ _ _ _ _ _ _ _ _ _ _

LOCATION 3: 6 markers

Bearings:
 90°
150°
210°
270°
330°
 30°
Shape? _ _ _ _ _ _ _ _ _ _ _ _ _ _ _

LOCATION 4: 8 markers

Bearings:
 90°
135°
180°
225°
270°
315°
360°
 45°
Shape? _ _ _ _ _ _ _ _ _ _ _ _ _ _ _

GROUP NAMES:

Orienteering (9)

Name -

Exercise – compass bearing orienteering
Look at the map provided by your teacher. You must visit checkpoints A to E in turn in a clockwise direction around the school field

At each checkpoint you must take the bearings listed below, locate the object on the bearing and write down the answer in the space provided

Accuracy is important

CHECKPOINT	BEARING	LANDMARK	BEARING	LANDMARK
A				
B				
C				
D				
E				

Exercise – compass bearings and pacing trail
Complete the trail, writing down the name of the locations at the end of each leg of the trail

Remember:

○ 1 pace = counting when only left or right leg comes forwards, e.g. L–R–L = 2 paces

○ Beware of roads – keep to the path

○ Each member of your group takes turns at each stage of the trail

START:

LEG   BEARING   PACES   LOCATION

GROUP NAMES:

Residential experience – camping and bivouacking

KS: 2/3

PoS: KS2: a, b, c; KS3: a, c, d

Aim: to promote teamwork and tolerance of others, and to provide a vehicle for residential experience. To develop camp-craft skills

Time required: one night (minimum)

Location: static camps on approved camp-sites or school field; bivouac sites close to human habitation in coastal/woodland environments

Resources: tents, stoves, fuel, bivouac materials ranging from plastic survival bags to poles, rope, polythene sheets, large stones

Target group: 11–12-year-olds. Groups of up to 30

Teacher's guidance notes

Note: A teacher wishing to embark on this type of activity should possess all the relevant campcraft skills. Numerous textbooks are available.

Camping is an extremely rewarding activity for promoting personal and social development – a highly effective form of residential experience. Children regard camping as an adventure, an opportunity for them to live out of doors.

A previous residential experience using a youth hostel or similar location may be advisable, as this will form a good introduction to residential experience before tackling the more demanding routines required in camping.

The camping trip may serve as a means of pursuing other activities such as day/night walks, orienteering or night lines. A night line is a rope line which is threaded through a forest for a distance of a 100m or so; the pupils have to follow the line on their own. Care must be taken to ensure that pupils cannot sustain eye damage – for instance, do not select a route which winds through densely overgrown vegetation. Make sure also that a member of staff is at the other end and possibly post another hidden helper somewhere along the route.

Startling children with spooky noises and movements is not to be recommended as it could have a detrimental effect. Attaching the rope(s) to trees with slings and climbing karabenas can help to maintain rope tension (tie off the rope at each karabena with a figure-of-eight knot).

Successful bivouacs and camps rely on good planning and preparation – not to mention good weather. Bivouacking is a good way of providing this type of experience when tents are not available or when a more adventurous outing is sought. Some local educational authorities operate a loan service: enquire via your PE adviser.

○ This form of residential experience should be confined to between April and October. Remember that days are short in April and October and frosty nights can be very cold under canvas.

○ Consult your local LEA's codes of practice for further guidance.

○ Adhere to the advice given in the section 'Planning a visit' (pages 81–5), especially regarding the close supervision of girls, pupil/staff ratios, staff gender for mixed groups and sanitary arrangements on sites with no facilities.

○ Ensure that all pupils have warm, waterproof clothing and all other items specified on the kit list.

○ For camps where the cooking is done on a communal basis, make sure the pupils know the routine for meals and chores. No activities should commence until all chores are completed. For camps where the children cook for themselves, each tent should operate as a separate unit.

○ Pre-visit training in campcraft skills as detailed in the pupil resources is essential.

○ Make sure that you have booked and visited the site before the visit.

○ Instil safety awareness regarding the dangers of cooking, contamination of food and fuel leakage.

○ Tents must be hung to dry back at base.

○ The staff must be aware of accident procedures and at least one member should be qualified in First Aid.

○ Obtain an up-to-date weather forecast, be prepared to abandon the activity or to seek better shelter if hostile weather is forecast.

Assessment: by direct observation in the field and by examination of responses to pupil resource material, questioning, feedback

Cross-curricular links: Environment; Health and Fitness; Citizenship; ICT; Food Technology

Pupil resources: *see* worksheets

Extension and Enrichment: where is the nearest camp site to your home?

Vocabulary: dehydrated, menu, calorific value, flysheet, bivouac, inflammable, toxic, shelter, back-packing, purification

KS2/3

Camping (1)

Name _____

Food for the camp

○ Your teacher may have decided that he or she will bring all the food for the group. If so, you will be informed of the menu

○ Are you a vegetarian? Do you have to have a special diet? If so, see your teacher and explain in good time for special arrangements to be made for you

○ If you are cooking your own food, you must decide on a common menu with the rest of your tent group, and decide who is going to bring what. Bear in mind what it's like trying to prepare food out of doors on a small camping stove. Your meals should be simple to prepare all at once in one pan (e.g. stew)

○ You do not need to bring any special dehydrated meals that are quite expensive to buy in outdoor shops. Tinned foods, pot noodles, packet soups, etc. will do fine because we don't have to worry about the weight in the same way as we would do if we were carrying the food and camping equipment on an expedition

○ Don't forget your tin opener, scouring pad, washing-up liquid and matches

○ Keep milk and other fresh food out of the sun

○ Try to bring food that will provide a high level of nutrition (protein) and energy (carbohydrate) to make up for the extra demands put on you during the activities

○ All foods have a 'calorific value': this is a measure of the energy they can provide in the form of sugar or fat. Cereals and fruit will help your digestion

○ The following foods are high in nutritional value and will provide you with a high-energy, balanced diet:

meat stew, soup, pasta, tea bags, SOYA MEAL, cheese, beans, MARG, salt, vegetables, COFFEE, bread, nuts, Cereal, rice, Crisps, dessert, milk, sugar, raisins, sultanas, dried fruit, potatoes

Camping (2)

Name _____

Cooking skills

Your teacher may have decided that there will be a 'cook tent' where all food is prepared by the staff and/or a group of pupils for the whole group. If, however, you are cooking for yourselves, you need to learn how to use a small camping stove. (Your teacher may ask you to bring one into school if you have your own.)

Remember that the flames from the burner can be very dangerous, especially those from pressure stoves and from stoves that use petrol. For our safety you will only be allowed to use stoves that use gas cartridges or methylated spirit fuel.

Your teacher will demonstrate and check that you know how to use your stove.

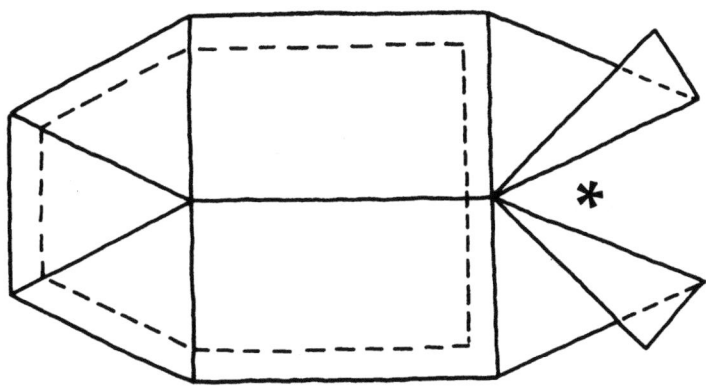

On no account cook inside the main tent. In bad weather, bring the stove inside the flysheet. But beware of flare-ups!

Rules

1 The stove must be in the mouth of the tent, as shown in the drawing above*

2 There must not be any spilt or spare fuel nearby

3 Only one person must cook; everyone else must sit still

4 Fill stoves outside the tent

5 Make sure that the fuel bottle and stove caps are secure

Exercise

Equipment required: camping stove and pan, clean water, teabags or coffee, milk, sugar, scouring pad, water container.

When your teacher has shown you how to use the stove, boil a pan of water and use it to make a cup of tea or coffee. When you have finished, clean up all your equipment with the scouring pad.

Camping (3)

Name _____

Campcraft skills

- Each tent or bivouac group should operate as a separate unit
- Only take those items on the equipment list
- Take a spare set of clothes in a plastic bag (this can also act as a pillow)
- Be settled in your tent or bivouac shelter and finish any cooking by nightfall if possible
- Hang wet tents to dry back at base to prevent rotting
- Always wash your hands before handling food, especially after visits to the loo or after handling fuel
- An insulation mat or airbed under your sleeping bag will keep you warmer and is more comfortable than sleeping on the ground
- Always sleep head-to-tail in small tents where there isn't much space

- Keep all rubbish in a dustbin or plastic carrier bags

Living in the tent in bad weather

The important point here is to reduce movement to a minimum

- Remove boots before placing feet on groundsheet
- Remove waterproofs outside; store them in a corner of the tent or underneath the flysheet
- Before settling down to cook, make sure that you have all you need, e.g. water for both cooking and washing up
- Try to keep the inside of the tent neat and organised
- In cold weather, stuff as much clothing and as many plastic bags, etc. as possible underneath your sleeping bag to insulate you from the cold ground

Hazards

- Tents are covered with inflammable material: don't have naked flames inside or close to the tent
- Never leave gas cylinders in the tent: a layer of toxic gas may build up overnight and suffocate you
- Always cook outside: bring the stove into the front of the tent in foul weather

LEAVE THE SITE CLEAN AND TIDY!

Camping and bivouacking

Name _____

○ Camping and bivouacking are great ways of living out of doors. They can be a lot of fun and a really memorable adventure, especially in the countryside at night

○ A bivouac is a shelter which will protect you from the wind and rain

○ We will have a better time if we learn how to keep ourselves warm, dry and comfortable, and make sure that our camping and bivouacking equipment is in good order before we leave the school. Our camp or bivouac activity will take place during the summer months – winter camping calls for more specialised equipment to keep you warm

○ Some outdoor adventurers like to carry their camping equipment with them on their journey, and possibly camp in wild, remote places. This is known as 'backpacking'. You may get the chance to make an expedition like this when you are older and stronger

○ We can use our camp as a base for other activities such as night lines, orienteering, and day or night hikes

○ We should always get permission from the camp site owner before we attempt to set up our tents or prepare a bivouac site. Approved camp sites will have clean water for drinking and cooking, toilets and washing facilities. Remember also that sound carries a long way out of doors, so try to be settled and quiet between 11pm and 7am

○ Camping and bivouacking in the wilds can be a great adventure, but again we must get permission first from the landowner and choose a site where we can get fresh water. The water should be crystal clear and free from any mud or smell. Clean water is difficult to find other than in the mountains, and even then it must be boiled or treated with purification tablets (which you can buy from chemists). It may be possible for your teacher to take the water with you in a large drum with a tap

○ If you are camping in the wilds you must also make your own arrangements for toilets, washing up and washing. Someone in the group must be prepared to dig a trench 150 cm deep for people to use to go to the toilet. Waste is covered as necessary with a trowel

What makes a good camp site?

Fill in and colour the spider chart with things that you feel make a good camp or bivouac site.

Now share these ideas with your teacher and the rest of the group. Extend the spider chart if necessary to add your teacher's answers.

150 cm

CAMP/
BIVOUAC SITE

Bivouacking

Name _____

○ To build a bivouac we need to use many of the skills we have learned for camping. However, we must now ask ourselves: How can we shelter from the wind and rain?

○ A bivouac bag – normally a man-size, orange-coloured plastic bag – makes an acceptable shelter. Mountaineers carry one for emergency use. However, you do tend to end up quite wet from condensation

○ Complete the spider chart below by inserting as many solutions as you can think of to the problem of providing shelter

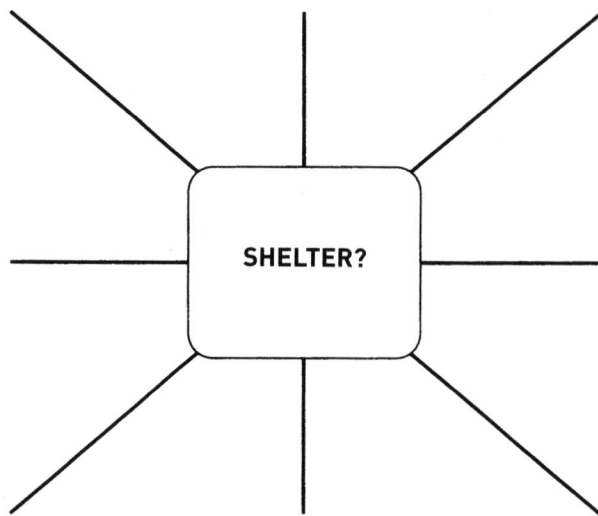

SHELTER?

○ Now let's go out on to the school field and prepare a bivouac shelter with the materials provided by your teacher

Problem-solving activities

KS: 2/3

PoS: KS2: a, b, c; KS3: a, b, c

Aim: to share ideas and work together on specified problems of a physical nature; to develop teamwork

Time required: each activity should start with a written brief of what is required of the group, followed by a 5-minute 'thinking time'. All the activities will run for about 30 minutes except raft building and rafting, which should be tackled in isolation over a period of 1–2 hours. The other activities can be arranged in a 'circus' system – over a two- or three-period session

Location: in the school grounds; on a slow-moving river or lakeside

Resources: *Centipede:* two planks, tape or rope slings. *Acid stream:* two planks, three acid-resistant pedestals (for example milk crates). *Square dance/Sheep in the pen:* rope, blindfolds. *Dots and lines:* 9 cones, rope. *Retrieving the bucket:* bucket, boundary rope, coils of rope long enough to span boundary, miscellaneous equipment not needed. *Reef knot around the tree:* rope. *Filling the leaking container:* large 'well' dustbin filled with water, leaking transporting swing bin, leaking dustbin to be filled. *Raft building and rafting on placid water*:* plastic/steel drums, planks/poles, rope, paddles/oars, buoyancy aids/life-jackets, helmets, inner tubes/tyres/polystyrene blocks. *Human crane:* Base line e.g. rope and planting stick

Target group: 11–13-year-olds

KS2/3

Teacher's guidance notes

Centipede

Pupil brief You are to use the planks and slings provided to move your team over the specified distance in the shortest possible time. The whole group must move together in formation with both feet in contact with the planks at all times.

Solution/teacher's notes

Slings used as handles to lift planks
Feet placed on each plank

Acid stream

Pupil brief Your group must cross the acid stream in the shortest possible time. The only acid-resistant equipment that you have are the three pedestals. If a member of the group falls into the stream, start again.

Solution/teacher's notes

Square dance

Pupil brief Assemble by the joined rope that has been laid out on the ground for you. Elect one member of your group to issue instructions. The remainder of the group then blindfold themselves. Only the leader may speak; he or she must get the rest of the group to form a square with the rope in the shortest possible time.

Any other member of the group attempting to use verbal communications will cause the group to have to start again.

KS2/3

Solution/teacher's notes

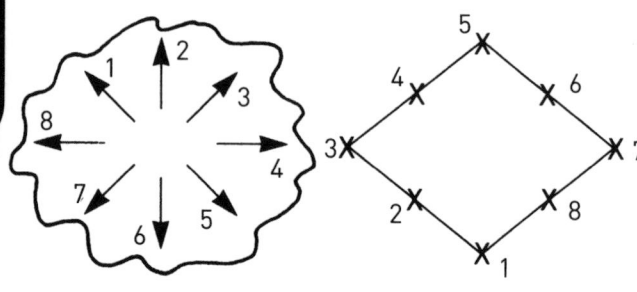

Retrieving the bucket

Pupil brief Using any of the equipment provided, devise a method of removing the bucket from the centre of the boundary circle – without trespassing inside – in the shortest possible time. If any member trespasses the group must start again.

Solution/teacher's notes

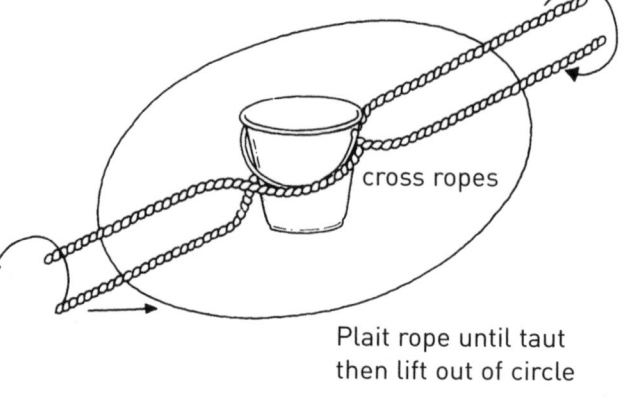

cross ropes

Plait rope until taut then lift out of circle

Dots and lines

Pupil brief Using the rope provided, devise a means of joining all the cones with four straight lines. You will be timed.

Solution/teacher's notes

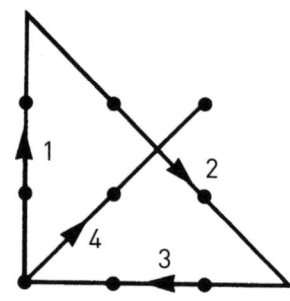

Reef knot around the tree

Pupil brief Look at the diagram of the reef knot tied around the tree. A reef knot is tied by 'over-left, over-right', then 'right over left'. Your group must use the rope provided to tie the reef knot around the tree in the shortest possible time. The rope is covered with glue so that once you pick it up you must remain in contact with it. If any member of the team lets go the group has to start again.

Solution/teacher's notes

Human Crane

Pupil brief Your task is to create a human crane to extend as far as possible beyond the datum line with the aim of inserting a stick into the ground. No part of anyone's body must make contact with the ground beyond the start line at any time. You must observe good lifting and injury prevention practices throughout.

Solution/teacher's notes

Sheep in the pen

Pupil brief Your task is to get your 'sheep' into the pen in the shortest possible time. You must elect one person to be the 'shepherd' who can only use commands of left, right, forwards, backwards, stop. Each sheep must have an individual name or number.

Solution/teacher's notes

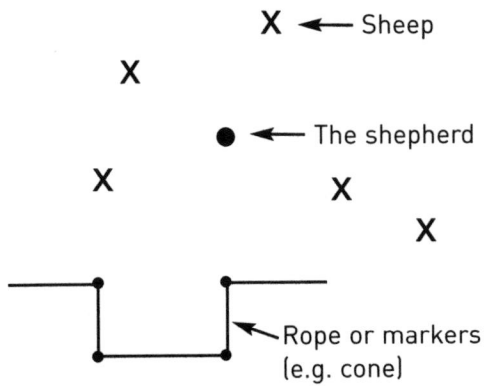

X ← Sheep

X

● ← The shepherd

X

Rope or markers (e.g. cone)

KS2/3

Filling the leaking container

Pupil brief Your team must attempt to fill the leaking dustbin with water transported in the leaking bucket. You will be timed and the height of water achieved will be measured.

Solution/teacher's notes
When drilling holes in the carrying vessel, drill them in such a manner that outspread fingers could 'plug' the holes. Some members of the group may use their fingers to plug holes.

Raft building and rafting on placid water

Pupil brief You are to build a raft and cross the expanse of water in front of you in the shortest possible time. You may use any of the materials provided. You must all wear a buoyancy aid/life-jacket and helmet before attempting to launch your craft.

Solution/teacher's notes
Raft building encourages the pupils to share their ideas and develop practical skills, improvising with given materials to create a seaworthy craft capable of crossing a stretch of placid water. The water must be placid, i.e. still or slow moving, for negotiating river currents and especially whitewater – of any description – requires the use of specialised inflatable rafts and a qualified helmsman.

A brief discussion on paddling skills before the exercise begins is useful. Perhaps you could liken the movements to those of a fish's fins: for example, 'flick the left fin and the fish will move to the right'; the tail or dorsal fin (the helmsman) provides the steerage. The helmsman gives commands, such as 'left forward', 'right back', 'forward together', 'reverse together', etc. to manoeuvre the craft.

You could also describe: sitting/kneeling/ standing positions on the raft; balancing and gripping the paddle; taking care with double-bladed canoe paddles not to hit people on the head; what to do if the raft becomes unseaworthy and the crew have to abandon ship. On small rivers where the bank is never too far away, pupils should swim on their back. On larger expanses of water, such as a lake, there should be a motorised power boat in attendance. Other factors such as surface drift and wind direction are significant.

Pupils could be given the task of getting from A to B using a set course (such as sailing markers). This activity is best reserved for the summer months to avoid any possibility of hypothermia through immersion in the water. Furthermore, I feel that this activity should only take place if a qualified RLSS lifesaver is in attendance.

An extension of this activity could include a visit to the white-water rafting centres in Bala, North Wales or in Nottingham.

Note A minimum swimming ability of 50 m is advised. If in doubt, contact your LEA advisor.

Assessment: by direct observation, questioning, feedback

Cross-curricular links: Technology; Language

Pupil resources: pupils need problem brief sheets adapted from text included above

Extension and Enrichment: try to devise a problem-solving activity of your own that involves teamwork

Vocabulary: command words, cones, reef knot, boundaries, pen, base line, helmsman, crew, trespass, crane, shepherd, raft, paddle, bank, currents, surface, drift

KS2/3

Planning a visit

Off-site visits for educational purposes are an accepted aspect of modern teaching. They are strategies for the reinforcement of subject matter studied in the classroom, a means of learning new skills and practising existing ones, of promoting PSHE and experiencing new environments. A school visit creates a great deal of excitement among young children so it can be used as a motivating force in the classroom. A visit will provide opportunities for implementing the process of physical education, namely:

1 **Acquiring and developing skills**: pupils can be involved in choosing clothing, footwear and equipment.

2 **Selecting and applying skills, tactics and compositional ideas**: plotting routes on maps, bringing food and finding out about the areas to be visited; also using the skills taught at school off-site in a different environment.

3 **Knowledge and understanding of fitness and health**: the need for the content of food and drinks to provide the necessary energy, nutrition and hydration while engaged in the activities. Recognising the need to regulate clothing according to the climatic conditions/level of physical activity. Personal hygiene and injury prevention (e.g. blisters). Learning to pace oneself to achieve optimum cardiovascular performance and avoid fatigue.

4 **Evaluating performance**: producing records and exhibitions; writing an account of activities

A school visit of any kind requires a lot of forethought and prior planning. Here is a list of factors to bear in mind when proposing an off-site experience for the pupils:

❍ Parents should be notified by formal letter with a reply slip and a medical consent form. The latter should ask for details of any medical condition that the supervising staff should know about, of any medication being taken and of the pupil's swimming ability. It should ask consent for emergency First Aid to be carried out if necessary. The telephone number of the family doctor, together with a contact telephone number and address, should also be obtained (see sample form on page 84, which may be photocopied if required).

The letter should outline the purpose of the trip, the cost, the planned activities, personal requirements regarding clothing, food, equipment and spending money, the departure time and meeting place and the estimated time of return (see sample letters on pages 84–85).

Regarding the cost of trips, legislation has deemed that if a visit takes place for the most part in curriculum time and is seen as part of the curriculum, then the school must fund the trip. Parents can be asked to provide voluntary contributions. If, however, the trip takes place for the large part in extra-curricular time (at the weekend), then the cost of the trip must be borne by the pupils. The school may make an extra charge for maintenance of equipment, staff INSET related to the activity, etc., but this must be clearly stated on the letter to the parents.

Always keep a record of all purchases with receipts. A balance sheet should be drawn up and submitted to the school Bursar after the trip. Do not forget that VAT is reclaimable for school trips.

❍ Always give pupils the opportunity to ring their parents when returning to school from a visit that has taken place in extra-curricular time. This will let parents know when to come to collect their children. If there is equipment to be stowed or unpacked then make allowances for this. Do not leave any pupils unattended, especially after dark, once the trip is over. If you are likely to be delayed, ring as soon as it is convenient.

❍ At motorway service areas, rest stops, etc. ask pupils to keep in groups of four. Give specific times of return (30 minutes is normally sufficient), no-go areas and cautions about strangers. Make sure that pupils know where the vehicle is in relation to the car park as a whole. Warn pupils about moving traffic within service areas (I also warn my pupils about spending too much money). At what age you allow your pupils to go unsupervised is a difficult question that can only be answered according to individual situations. Finally, make sure the pupils know where you will be in an emergency.

❍ Long journeys can be very frustrating for children. I try to stop every couple of hours, preferably at a point where there is something interesting to look at or do (the French auto-route rest stops are well ahead of us in this respect). On extremely long journeys, an overnight stay will be required – an opportunity to make a standing camp, to bivouac, or find a youth hostel. I always look for accommodation that will not hinder the journey a great deal. Some trips using coach travel require pupils to sleep through the night while travelling. Travelling through the night can itself be a big adventure for children.

Finally, on long journeys, always make generous allowances for travelling times. Rushing to meet deadlines is both dangerous and mentally exhausting. Gone are the days when motorway travel was fast and smooth!

○ For any visit, consultation should first take place with the head teacher and possibly the Educational Visits Coordinator (EVC). Visits requiring an overnight stay are classified as a residential visit, and some LEAs have a form which must be completed for such trips. However, with schools becoming more and more accountable for themselves, many schools are devising their own application forms.

○ It may be wise to take out an insurance policy for the visit through the LEA insurers in order to cover the pupils for accidents, loss of personal belongings, liability, etc. Staff are covered for third party liability as employees of the authority, provided that they are acting with the consent of the head teacher and operating within accepted codes of practice. A copy of the LEA's code of practice for educational visits and outdoor pursuits should be available from your head teacher, EVC or PE/O.Ed adviser.

○ Transporting a group has become quite complicated with the recent legislation relating to minibuses. In most cases your school's insurance will require you to have a clean licence and to be over 25 years of age in order to drive. For most operating authorities the driver(s) will also need to have undertaken training through the Transportation dept to gain a 'MIDAS' mini-bus driver's licence. The bus will need to carry a Bus Permit (available to all schools free of charge). The bus will have a log book which must be completed for every journey – a tedious business, but one which is essential if you are to remain within the law. Tachographs will soon be compulsory for Britain to fall in line with the rest of the EC. The minibus must have a side door for passenger access/exit, especially if a trailer is being towed. If you are driving abroad,

please consult your local authority on other documents you may need to carry. There are also recommendations relating to the availability of a mobile phone on minibus journeys of two or three hours. Consult your local authority for more details on this and also on towing a trailer. Also, if towing a trailer the rear doors must not be obstructed. No luggage, e.g. rucksacks, must be loaded inside the vehicle unless strapped down – approved nets are available, or a roofrack is another option; however, they in themselves are fraught with dangers for the unwary.

Driver's times and the number of drivers relating to distance travelled are also prescribed in the MIDAS regulations.

○ It is very important to observe recommended pupil/staff ratios, which for most visits will be 15:1. To have two members of staff is safer. For hazardous outdoor activities the ratios drop dramatically. Your codes of practice will provide guidance.

○ Pupils should be fully briefed prior to the visit regarding what will constitute acceptable conduct and what will not. It can be useful to include this in the parents' letter. With younger children there are likely to be fewer problems than with, say, 11-year-olds.

○ A pre-visit by the supervising staff is highly recommended in order to rehearse the activity; seek out provision for toilets, lunch spots, parking, access, alternative bad weather activities/routes, etc. In the case of potentially hazardous outdoor pursuits, the implications for the supervising staff if an accident occurred and no pre-visit had been made are very grave.

○ Always try to find out what the weather is going to be like and change your plans to suit. For example, it is no good trying to introduce canoeing to a novice group on a river in flood. The weather may have a marked effect on the safety of the activity: rocks become slippery to climb in the wet, and strong winds can sap one's strength.

○ Have carried out necessary risk assessments for the activity and, if Category C, have had them approved by the LEA advisor.

○ *Leader's skills*:

a Always appoint another member of staff to bring up the rear and keep the group together. There should be regular 'head counts'. Large groups should be sub-divided into smaller groups with a member of staff for each group.

b At least one member of staff should be a qualified first aider through the St. John Ambulance or a similar organisation. I have included a section on emergency First Aid under the supervision and safety section of the book (see pages 52 and 86–91).

c Understand what to do in an emergency and how to effect improvised evacuations. Again I have included these skills in the supervision and safety section.

d Have a good practical knowledge of navigation techniques.

○ *Extra considerations for residential trips*:

a For mixed residentials it is recommended that there is a male member of staff for boys and a female member of staff for girls.

b Extra supervision is required for young pupils and girls.

c There may need to be a member of staff responsible for management of pupils' spending money. Records should be kept in these cases.

d What provision is being made for the evenings? Organised activities or free time?

e Will the children be allowed to go unsupervised off-site? At what times? Under what conditions? Where may they go and what may they do?

f If the residential is camp-based, then it should take place between the months of April and October – bearing in mind that spring and autumn days are short, and the nights long and cold!

As stated in Chapter 1, a government enquiry into a number of recent tragedies has recommended that every LEA now appoints a safety officer for off-site visits/trips as should schools (EVC), plus each member of staff should be equipped with a safety handbook.

Planning a visit (1)

Sample consent form

Activity leader _____ **Pupil's name** _____

School address _____ **Address** _____

_____ _____

_____tel _____ _____tel _____

Activity _____ **Dates** _____

Dear _____

1 I hereby give consent for my son/daughter to attend adventure-based outdoor activities organised on behalf of the school.

2 I understand that these activities have inherent 'potential' dangers and, while the staff in charge of the party will take all reasonable care of the children, the staff cannot necessarily be held responsible for any loss, damage or injury suffered by my son/daughter arising during or out of the school journey; unless the staff are found to be negligent in their duties.

3 I accept the extent of the personal insurance arrangements made by, or on behalf of, the leaders of this activity, to cover the party for expenses for medical requirements and unavoidable cancellation, and insurance for personal accident, personal effects and third party. *Note: further details of the policies may be obtained from the activity leader.*

4 National Health Service **Doctor's name** _____

   Doctor's tel _____

5 I certify that my son/daughter is/is not subject to:

   ○ heart disease ○ asthma

   ○ respiratory disease ○ any other complaint or allergies

   ○ epilepsy (please state) _____

6 My son/daughter is/is not required to take any medication. I will ensure he/she takes an adequate supply. (Please state medication, times of dose, reason for taking medication.)

   _____

7 I consent to any emergency medical treatment necessary in the case of illness/accident during the course of the activities.

8 Can your son/daughter swim 50 m in light clothing? (This is a pre-requisite for acceptance on water-based activities.) YES/ NO

Signed (Parent/Guardian) _____ **Date** _____

Planning a visit (2)

Sample letter

Dear Parent/Guardian

WHITEWATER KAYAKING: date of trip _

I shall be organising a whitewater kayaking trip to the river Derwent at Matlock, Derbyshire. The cost is £10.00 to cover the cost of minibus hire, staff training and maintenance of equipment.

We shall be leaving the school at 9.00am and hopefully returning at about 7.00pm. This trip is not suited to beginners (BCU 2 Star is the minimum standard). Previous experience of kayaking on flat water is essential. Your son/daughter must be able to swim. If in doubt, please contact me.

Your son/daughter will need to bring a change of clothes, towel, lunch and drink. The following is required for the kayaking: training shoes, thermal/cotton T-shirt, warm socks/wetsuit boots, sweatshirt or fleece garment, and a wetsuit if available. There should be an opportunity to visit other facilities at the water-sports centre during the day.

I must know if your son/daughter suffers from heart disease, asthma, epilepsy or any other complaint that may be aggravated by immersion in cold water. Please note that if your son/daughter becomes unwell following immersion in river water, you should contact your doctor. There is the very remote chance of catching Weil's Disease which has been known to be fatal if left untreated.

Please return the slip below, together with payment and the attached medical consent form.

Yours sincerely

D. Balazik AD.DIP.O.ED.
Head of Outdoor Pursuits
BCU L3 Kayak Coach (A3* Assessor)

....

Name of student _

I wish my son/daughter to take part in the whitewater kayaking trip. I enclose a cheque for £10.00 made payable to Sponne School.

Signed _(Parent/Guardian)

Supervision and safety

In promoting an outdoor adventure activity the supervising teachers must accept that they are ultimately responsible for the safety and welfare of the pupils. If an outside agency is taking responsibility for the activity then to some extent the level of accountability is diminished, but it may be argued that the contracting of the outside agency has been the responsibility of the teacher organising the activity on behalf of the school and its pupils. Further advice and information on the latter is given on pages 92–3.

I would always advise teachers to work strictly within the guidelines set by your LEA to ensure that a claim of negligence would be difficult to uphold in the event of a mishap.

In the case of hazardous outdoor pursuits (climbing, abseiling, zip wires and aeriel ropeways, canoeing, sail-based activities, mountain-based activities, air-based activities, sub-aqua, etc.), the LEA has a duty to ensure that adequate INSET programmes are available where required or to acknowledge national qualifications (NGBs) and experience. Some LEAs operate a log-book accreditation scheme for teachers wishing to introduce these activities at a 'taster' level. The national qualifications are really aimed at those individuals who are in an overall position of responsibility or who are seeking professional, vocational status in this area of educational experience. National qualifications for the most part assume previous experience and personal competence, and are expensive and time consuming. Teachers who are suitably trained and working within the codes of practice should be covered by the LEA for third party claims of negligence.

General points regarding safety

1 Supervising staff should take steps to acquaint themselves fully with potential risk situations involved in a particular activity, and to devise approved strategies to combat the danger. These may include:

   a eliminating the risk by changing or modifying your plans

   b reducing the risk by increasing the supervision

   c using appropriate safety equipment that is in good order (climbing equipment in particular requires close scrutiny and maintenance). Contact the relevant governing body for the sport for further advice. Addresses from the Sports Council

   d psychological/physical support

2 Try to make sure that any venture you organise is flexible and carefully structured. Do not leave things to chance! Ensure that the activity has been 'rehearsed' at the designated venue where practicable.

3 You should always operate in such a way that you yourself are confident in any situations that the activity may present.

4 You should be aware of and well-practised in emergency procedures.

5 Has the activity been pitched at the correct mental/physical level for the group?

6 Is the group too large?

7 Is there an escape plan?

8 Where close supervision is not possible, such as during orienteering in a forested area, then the pupils require briefing in an emergency plan. For example, in the event of an accident, leave one person with the casualty, keep them warm, send two people to base or summon help with distress signals.

You should always be prepared to answer the following questions:

1 Does the activity have a purpose and desirable educational aim?

2 Am I fit emotionally/physically to lead this activity?

3 Do I have the necessary technical skills and experience?

4 Am I working within LEA guidelines and my qualifications/experience?

5 Have the pupils been briefed in an accident plan where needed? Do I have the necessary First Aid kit/training to deal with any mishap?

6 Do I know how to effect a rescue?

7 Do the pupils have the physical/mental attributes to cope with the activity? Have they received adequate training?

8 Have the parents completed a consent form and medical questionnaire? Is the approval of a doctor required for any of the pupils?

9 Are the pupils aware of their own limitations and capabilities?

10 Are the pupils equipped nutritionally and clothed adequately for the activity?

11 Do the pupils have the correct personal equipment for the activity? Have they been trained in its usage?

12 Do the pupils understand the purpose of the activity?

13 Is the size of the group appropriate (consider the aims and nature of the activity, the need for communication, management, rescue and evacuation)?

14 Are you familiar with the area to be visited and effects of bad weather on the nature of the terrain (for example, bad visibility on featureless moorland, heavy rainfall creating swollen rivers)?

15 Is the venue sufficiently remote to create difficulties in getting to help in an emergency – where is the nearest telephone?

16 Do you need to leave details of your activity with someone who can contact emergency services if required? N.B. Always remember to make contact on your safe return!

17 Are you using public rights of way (PROW) for your activity; are you trespassing? Have you a legal right to access/exit on any water you may be using?

18 Are you and the pupils aware of any conservation issues that are relevant to the activity (for example, Country Code, footpath erosion)?

19 Are the pupils briefed as to any viral infections that may be contracted from activities involving water (for example Weil's Disease)?

Supervision tips

1 Be friendly but firm.

2 Insist on quietness and on the pupils' full, undivided attention when giving instruction. At some off-site venues there are often distractions out of one's control: wait until they have passed, or choose a new spot for briefing.

3 Keep the group together. Lead from the front. Do not let any pupil force the pace. I sometimes put the weakest member of the party at the front with me and let them set the pace, including rest stops. This gives the weaker ones more incentive.

4 Address any negative comments by pupils immediately before they escalate. Do not tolerate chastisement of pupils by other pupils. Reprimand silly, irresponsible actions; threaten to terminate the pupils' involvement or to curtail the activity if it continues (this normally works if you have got the activity right!).

5 Ensure that your assistant(s) are fully briefed. One should act as a 'tail-end Charlie' to keep the group together.

6 By keeping your group together you will avoid losing members, and prevent exhaustion or disillusionment.

7 When giving a demonstration or passing on instruction, make sure that the group can see and hear you. Don't take it for granted – ask them. Try to position yourself so that the sun is not in their eyes. On windy days try to position yourself upwind.

8 Keep descriptions and demonstrations as brief as possible. Don't waffle on! Don't try to teach too much at once. There are a number of good instructional strategies in common use:

EDICT: Explanation, Demonstration, Imitation, Correction, Testing

IDEAS: Introduction, Demonstration, Explanation, Activity, Summary

A good maxim for all of us involved in communicating information might be:

KISS: Keep It Simple and Safe

9 Make your demonstrations slow and deliberate. If you have ever watched a good ski instructor at work, you will notice how smooth and pronounced the actions are. Break down a procedure into progressive steps. Make sure the group can see clearly what you are doing – ask them: 'Can you see what I am doing?' Ensure that the sun is not in their eyes.

10 All voluntary leaders should be vetted for child abuse and a past history of criminal behaviour by submitting a police vetting form (CRB).

11 All leaders should be given support training and practical advice on how to recognise and deal with potential child abuse cases. Leaders should also think carefully about their own actions and not expose themselves to situations where allegations of child abuse could be made.

12 We have a duty to inform and direct our charges in good 'Manual Handling and Injury Prevention' techniques. The British Canoe Union produce a very good leaflet on this topic.

General safety skills and additional knowledge for supervisors of KS2 and KS3 activities

For hazardous outdoor pursuits you will need to seek further training.

For off-site activities you will need a First Aid pack containing: sterile dressings, bandage, triangular bandage (x2), antiseptic cream, scissors, antiseptic wipes, tape, salt tablets (for heat-related conditions), high-energy tablets, chocolate bars, Kendal mint cake (available from outdoor shops), antihistamine cream (for insect bites and stings), muscular rub (for strains and sprains) and vinyl disposable goves (hypoallergenic). Be aware that some students may be allergic to creams, plasters and latex. Also, the law prevents us from administering paracetamol etc.

In addition to the above, for activity A6 (camping and bivouacking) I would carry puritabs (available from chemists or outdoor shops) to purify water, and diocalm for upset stomachs.

For activity A5 (walks and rambles) I would also carry:

◯ a safety rope (30–45 m). This could be a 7–9 mm diameter hillwalker's safety rope or a 10/11 mm climber's rope – heavier, but also useful for climbing. This could be used to construct an improvised evacuation stretcher, improvised carries, or to cross a river

◯ a bivouac bag for treatment of hypothermia (a plastic survival bag is inexpensive and available from outdoor shops)

◯ an emergency stove for treatment of hypothermia. A small, portable affair that burns methylated spirit or camping gas is ideal

◯ a box of lifeboat waterproof matches

◯ a sugary powdered drink

◯ spare boot laces

◯ notepad for messages, a pencil and coins for telephone. All stored in plastic sandwich bags

◯ mobile phone

◯ protractor-based navigating compass (basic model is adequate)

Precautions for coastal/cliff walk activities

1 Keep the group well away from the edge of cliffs, especially in windy weather. Gusts can be fatal!

2 Instruct the children not to wander off on their own.

3 Do not allow climbing of cliffs. However, climbing over large rocks or along the base of the cliffs can be very enjoyable. A word of caution here: ask yourself if the rocks above are loose, if there are any warning notices about climbing on the rocks, and if you are in danger of becoming cut off by the incoming tide.

4 Note the weather forecast for the area, especially any warnings of strong winds or gales which will make the sea rough.

Keep the children well away from the water in rough conditions in case they are caught by a wave and swept out to sea. Rocky shores are particularly dangerous as the waves can rebound off the rocks. Sadly – as if one needed to be convinced of these dangers – one is reminded of the Land's End tragedy in which a group of school children were swept to their deaths while beachcombing in heavy seas. Harbour walls and exposed sea fronts or piers can present similar dangers.

Beaches can present other dangers such as undertows and rip tides (see 'The Seashore Safety Code', pages 33–35). If water-based activities are planned, such as swimming, snorkelling or canoeing, seek advice about the conditions and choose sheltered sites where help is at hand if needed. Ensure that you have the necessary training and experience to lead the activity, that the group is not extended beyond its abilities, that the equipment used is suited to the activity and that you and the group know what to do in an emergency. Do not under-estimate the power of the sea; it can cause you to lose control of an activity with disastrous con-sequences. If you are in any doubt about the conditions, contact the coastguard.

5 Do not allow children to sit under the base of cliffs unless you are sure that there is no loose rock which may tumble down.

6 'Coasteering' is a relatively new form of coastal adventure activity whereby pupils are set numerous challenges involving abseiling, climbing, swimming and jumping in the sea from rocky platforms.

Qualified, experienced personnel with life-saving abilities, a rescue boat and prior know-ledge of the area are essential for this hazardous adventure activity. Pupils should be equipped with wet suits, buoyancy aids, climb-ing harnesses and helmets.

There is no substitute for a proper course of training in First Aid. The following is a brief look at some of the common problems that you are likely to have to deal with:

Heat exhaustion (hypothermia)

The effects of excessive heat can be quite deva-stating. Heat exhaustion is brought about by loss of body fluids and salts through profuse sweating. Victims are generally unaware of their condition.

If the condition has been brought on by water deficiency, the victim will complain of acute thirst, fatigue and giddiness. The pulse will be rapid and the victim will have a high temperature. Treat the victim by giving sips of water at first then as much as required.

If the condition has been brought on by salt deficiency, the victim will exhibit the above symptoms (but the temperature will be normal) and also complain of muscle cramp. Salt in the form of a salty drink or as tablets should be administered to restore the balance.

Heat stroke

This is a serious extension of heat exhaustion. The symptoms are very similar to those of hypothermia (slurred speech, aggression, poor vision, etc.). The skin appears very hot and dry (no sweating). Other symptoms may be observed as for heat exhaustion.

Treatment is as for heat exhaustion plus fanning and sponging with cold water. If possible, immerse the victim in cold water, but do this gradually otherwise the shock may be fatal.

Cold exhaustion (hypothermia)

This extremely dangerous condition is caused by a lowering of the body's core temperature. It is also known as exposure.

Causes: immersion in cold water, exposure to chilling wind and rain, inadequate clothing, fatigue, injury, lack of energy-giving food. Children and the elderly are more susceptible than others.

Signs and symptoms: impaired vision, shivering, difficulty in breathing, abnormal heart rate, slurred speech, irrational behaviour. Collapse and uncon-sciousness (a serious deterioration leading to death within hours) will result if the symptoms are ignored. The casualty is often unaware of his condition.

Treatment: rest and keep warm. Offer warm sugary drinks if conscious, and reassure. Try to replace any wet clothes with spare dry clothing; place the victim in a sleeping bag if available and an emergency shelter such as a tent, plastic survival bag or any natural shelter available.

Consider exposure victims as invalids even if their condition improves. Do not rub the skin or give the patient alcohol as this will draw blood and body heat away from the inner core. Rapid re-warming should also be avoided. Immersion in a hot bath or shower is acceptable for victims with mild exposure. Severe cases of exposure should be evacuated to safety as soon as possible. Shock may develop in some casualties. Apply expired air resuscitation if breathing fails; external cardiac compression may be necessary in extreme cases.

Unconscious patient

Check for a response by shouting, pinching or shaking the victim. Next check ABC (Airway? Breathing? Circulation?).

Treatment: Expired air resuscitation and external cardiac compression (not to be practised on a live person – always use mannequins).

Frostnip and frostbite

This condition is an indication that the central core is drawing on all its blood supply to conserve body temperature. It is the result of a lack of blood in constricted blood vessels due to low temperatures. Exposure can develop quite easily from here.

Frostnip and the progression to frostbite affects the extremities which offer the least resistance to chilling (nose, mouth, fingers, toes, ears). Frostbite can lead to the loss of limbs and death through gangrene.

Frostnip signs and symptoms: whiteness and numbness in the affected parts, localised pain.

Treatment: re-warm affected parts as quickly as possible on a warm part of the body; put on insulated clothing or use the warmth from a fire.

Frostbite signs and symptoms: treatment for frostnip is ineffective. Frostbite results in immobility of affected parts, discoloration (blue or black), dead tissue and blisters.

Treatment: if re-warming is carried out it should be done rapidly and only if there is no chance of re-freezing occurring. In the field it is wise to immobilise the affected part, protect from further cooling and exposure before evacuating to base as quickly as possible.

When back at base, immerse the affected part in a hot bath for about 20 minutes or re-warm from indirect sources such as an electric fire. Do not prick blisters, do not rub the skin, do not give the victim alcohol and do not apply heat from solid objects.

Shock

Caused by a loss of fluid from the body, normally through loss of blood.

Signs and symptoms: pale complexion, confused state of mind, sweating, rapid but weak pulse.

Treatment: lay victim down, cover with blanket, elevate legs, reassure.

Burns

Immerse the affected part in cold water if possible. Do not prick blisters. Apply a sterile dressing and treat for shock. Severe burns may reduce the body fluid levels; in these cases it may be advisable to give the casualty drinks to restore fluid levels.

Finally, try to protect the affected area from further injury.

Sunburn

Move the victim into the shade and apply calamine lotion to the affected areas. Liquid intake will reduce dehydration.

Dislocations and sprains

Use a triangular bandage to immobilise the injured limb and evacuate to base. A cold compress is useful to reduce swelling. A crêpe bandage is useful for sprains.

Fractures

Immobilise and treat for shock. Only apply traction if the circulation to the limb has been cut off. Do not move anyone with a suspected fractured spine unless their life is threatened. In the case of the latter a large team of helpers is required to lift and support the victim along the whole length of the body. Avoid twisting.

Stings

Remove the sting and treat with antihistamine cream immediately.

Bites

Snake bite: The only poisonous snake in Great Britain is the adder. Unfortunately, it is common in upland areas. Treat the victim for shock and attempt to draw out the venom from the wound by washing it and applying antiseptic. Seek immediate help and commence expired air resuscitation if necessary.

Dog bite: treat the bite as one would do for an ordinary wound. Seek medical assistance when possible to guard against rabies.

Seasickness

A common problem when kayaking on the sea is rough conditions! Raft up and comfort the victim, lower the head towards the front of the kayak. Get to solid ground as soon as possible. Travel sickness pills taken prior to the journey may be advisable for those prone to seasickness.